Inspired Work

INSPIRED WORK

A New Testament Guide to Working with Purpose

Book and Study Guide

SCOTT ORTEGA

WESTBOW
P R E S S
A DIVISION OF THOMAS NELSON

ISBN: 978-1-4497-2123-7 (e)
ISBN: 978-1-4497-2058-2 (sc)
ISBN: 978-1-4497-2059-9 (hc)
Library of Congress Control Number: 2011932761

Printed in the United States of America
WestBow Press rev. date: 9/06/2011

WestBow Press books may be ordered through booksellers or by contacting:

WestBow Press
A Division of Thomas Nelson
1663 Liberty Drive
Bloomington, IN 47403
www.westbowpress.com
1-(866) 928-1240

For my boys, Kyle, Jake, and Lucas.
May they always view their jobs in the proper light.

Contents

Introduction   xv
That Other Place   xvii

Part I
Finding Inspiration 1

    I. It Starts With Faith 3

    II. Share the Love 11

    III. All Christians Are Leaders 16

Part II
Inspired Behavior 25

    IV. The Servant Leader 27

    V. Communities Are the Ultimate Teams ... 38

    VI. Communication Counts 46

    VII. Endurance 'til the End 51

Afterword   57

Study Guide

Introduction   **63**

Study Session 1
The Universal Truth 67

Study Session 2
Faith Applies to All We Do 75

Study Session 3
Faith and Submission to God's Will 78

Study Session 4
All with Love 84

Study Session 5
Faith Trumps Law 88

Study Session 6
All Christians Are Called to Be Leaders 94

Study Session 7
Faith Is an Active State 98

Study Session 8:
Servant Leadership 105

Study Session 9
Strength in Weakness 111

Study Session 10
One Community 115

Study Session 11
Good Communities Communicate..120

Study Session 12

Hope and Endurance 124

Final Study Session:

Baptism and the Holy Spirit...131

About the Author   140

Appendix A   141
Additional Resources   141

References   142

Glossary of Bible Translations Referenced for Quoted Verses	
NIV	New International Version
NLT	New Living Translation
RSV	Revised Standard Version

Please note: All verses referenced in this book have been sourced from the New International Version of the Bible unless otherwise noted at the end of the quote.

Additional study information and tools can be found at the author's website, *www.Inspired-Work.com.*

Preface

This book is intended to share scriptural truths that will help professed Christians better understand how increased reliance on their faith can improve their job satisfaction and performance. The primary premise is that by approaching their work so it contributes to the achievement of their life's overriding purpose, they can find lasting fulfillment.

We all know that our jobs are transient, eventually going away all together. Therefore, it is evident that our most deeply held values need to transcend our time at work. For me, however, "knowing" did not fully translate to "living" until very recently. It was the decision to actually take the step to re-establish a solid foundation to guide all parts of my life—beginning at home but also extending to how I approach my career—that gave rise to this book.

Don't expect to find a how-to book between these covers. I don't provide a long list of management tools or effective habits, and I don't provide available options on how you can assert yourself at work. Instead, the focus of this book is to highlight faith-based teachings that can help you find the inspiration for *why* you should make specific choices at work. After internalizing these scriptural truths and learning to look to them for motivation, I trust you will find outward applications in your professional career that best fit your own situation and style. But the starting point for all you do is accepting your faith.

With that in mind, Part I begins by drawing on the New Testament to identify values and beliefs in the Christian faith that readily lend themselves to guiding our interactions at work. The central concepts detailed in the chapters of Part I relate to defining how hope, love, and belief interact to inspire our behavior from the inside-out. Together, they represent principles of the Christian faith that are applicable to everyone, not just managers but all employees in all lines of work.

In Part II you will find a few leadership applications that directly arise from holding true to the values and beliefs discussed in Part I. Although the actual list of applications is endless, I have chosen to focus on some behaviors that, through experience, I've repeatedly seen can have broad impact. They are adopting a servant leadership mind-set, creating a community, fostering positive communication, and deriving strength from challenge. Letting your faith surface as these positive actions will provide you a wave of momentum that also will carry into other parts of your work.

As you read through the book, I hope the Bible verses I've highlighted resonate with you as much as they have with me; I hope they will pique your desire to make your faith central to your inspiration at work. To help you get as much as possible out of your reading experience, you also will find a companion study guide located on pages 61-139 of this book. Each study session provides additional Bible verses that will lead to a more in-depth appreciation of how the themes covered are interwoven throughout the New Testament. I believe you will find the real value of this book by reflecting on the Bible verses in the study guide. I strongly encourage you to read the study sessions as they are called out.

In all cases, keep in mind that I am not a formally trained biblical scholar, so if what I've written does not ring true with you, please remember to reflect on the Scriptures that anchor each chapter and study session. Better yet, go to the source and read it in context from the original authors. My intent is for you to discover your real inspiration in God's Word, not my words.

Finally, I'd like to give heartfelt thanks to the people who got me to this point in my journey to become more faith-led in all my activities. Dave Ferguson, lead pastor of Christian Community Church in Naperville, Illinois, and Troy McMahon, now lead pastor at Restore Community Church in Kansas City, Missouri, helped start the process by challenging my wife and me to join our first small group seven years ago, led by Kim and Mike Brown, who really helped us understand the value of linking ourselves to the broader Christian community. Dave also deserves credit for introducing me to Jim Galvin of Jim Galvin and Associates, who guided me through the Christian publishing landscape.

Long-time friends Kyle Reynolds and Hal Oates graciously provided objective feedback of early drafts, which is reflected in the final product. Additionally, Ben Davis, lead pastor, and Steve Widmer, Mike Lentz, Kirk Poser, David Weber, David Kowal, John Howard, Ken Dressler, and the entire staff and men's fraternity ministry at River Glen Church outside Waukesha, Wisconsin, are also deserving of special thanks for bringing me to this stage in my personal growth, where I am much more appreciative of the meaning and value of the Christian faith I had long taken for granted. Not only did they give me the renewed conviction that led to my recommitting through baptism, but they also provided invaluable support and feedback that helped me find the energy to publish this book to assist others who are at a similar transition point in their lives. It is refreshing to finally "step out of the boat!"

Behind everything, my wife, Cindi, deserves my love and gratitude. The fact she positively embraced my taking more than a year to research and pull this book and its companion study guide together—during a time between corporate jobs, when we had no real income, and an unexpected economic downturn slashed our savings—was a testament to me of the peace we all can find by trusting God's plan ahead of our own desires or fears. To this day, I am both amazed and appreciative of the balance she helped our family maintain during what otherwise could have been perceived as very trying times. Instead, we fondly remember this time as a couple of our best years.

Thanks to the support of the abovementioned people I stepped out of my comfort zone, despite being newly immersed in my Christian journey, to share these thoughts with you. My prayer is that it will also help you to establish a good starting point for furthering your own spiritual growth. If you have the faith, you have the means.

John 14:6.
Jesus answered, "I am the way and the truth and the life. No one comes to the Father except through me."

Now let's go to work.

Accept the Truth

Fundamental to being a Christian is belief in the undeniable truth of God's Word and the role Jesus plays in our ultimate salvation. The challenge is to make your views fit God's model, not to make his words fit your perception of the world.

Remember who has the perfect view of the big picture across time, borders, and viewpoints.

Go to study guide:
Introduction, page 61.
Session #1, The Universal Truth, page 66.

Introduction

Off to Work

That Other Place

Work. The word gives rise to many visceral interpretations, mostly independent of and often in opposition to the word "life." This is reflective of the amount of time and effort we have put into building and reinforcing the wall between our time at work and the rest of our day-to-day life.

As we toil for our income, we learn to categorize work as a necessity that competes for our time and attention. Common phrases like "Finding the perfect work/life balance" and "That's my job, not me" suggest we accept a pervasive conflict between our personal lives and our work lives. Thus, we opt to treat them as distinctly separate facets of our day, which results in our trying to live a dual-purpose life governed by opposing values and beliefs.

The forces that motivate us to park our faith at the door as we leave home for work are very powerful. They're also very damaging to our real value as Christians and employees. By forcing distinction between our faith and our job, we actually limit the potential we have to fully enjoy the benefits of our strongest asset: our faith.

Even when we find our faith central to our family's well-being, we have a tendency to interpret society's common desire to maintain complete separation between religion and work as a need to also keep our internalized faith dormant on the job. As a result, we choose to err on the side of mirroring the established culture of the organization, instead of finding the motivations for our actions in the values and beliefs espoused by our faith. Whether driven by a hunger for advancement, a desire to be liked, or the influence of situational pressures, we become chameleons and adapt to the colors of the group with whom we work.

At other times, we may feel we are under the aegis of senior leadership. We surrender control of our work environment and personal actions to the corporate powers that be so we can be seen as good employees. Accepting direction from above makes it easier to blend in without taking full responsibility for the consequences—or so we rationalize.

In the early 1960s, psychologist Stanley Milgram performed several experiments at Yale University that illustrate the negative potential of ambivalently accepting direction from one's employers. In his research

Milgram structured an experiment in a lab, where the test subjects were ordinary citizens seated at a fake electric-shock machine. They were told to shock what appeared to be participants in a memory test every time the participants got an answer wrong. For each wrong answer, the voltage applied increased by fifteen volts. After thirty mistakes, the subject delivered a maximum shock of 450 volts to the helpless victims. Fortunately, the memory test participants were really actors, and the electrical shock was only imaginary. But the willingness of the subjects to mete out severe punishment on command was very real.

In the end, 65 percent of the test subjects completed the entire test, weathering the actors' screams and pleas to stop the experiment and continuing to increase the voltage, even after the actors fell silent. When asked why they would knowingly inflict increasing levels of pain to the innocent participants, despite the participants' obvious fear and distress, the test subjects' rationale basically came down to acceptance of authority. All it took was a white lab coat, the right situation, and someone they had just met convinced them to set aside their conscience.

Stanley Milgram's experiments and others like them help demonstrate that otherwise good citizens will willingly participate in abhorrent behavior, given the right situation. This ability for us, as humans, to rationalize a disconnect between what we know to be right and our actual actions has been replicated in other controlled studies, following Stanley Milgram's efforts. However, because of the adverse effects the tests had on the test subjects, many of whom suffered lasting depression and guilt, such tests are no longer allowed to go to the same extremes to prove we are capable of adopting evil on command.

Instead, we only have to look at the world around us to understand the fragile line between obeying our own conscience and joining someone else's nightmare. Evidence abounds of broadly supported genocides throughout recent times, including the Jews during World War II, Tutsis in Rwanda, Kurds in Iraq, and Muslims in Serbia. The list continues. Were all those who participated in such atrocities devils, or did many categorically set aside their values due to external influences?

These are extreme examples, but they are mentioned to raise our awareness that we have to be vigilant and remain receptive to the guidance of the Holy Spirit when we are subject to external influences, especially in situations where we might easily act upon flawed inclinations. Otherwise, we risk erroneously adopting that which is thrust upon us, regardless of its nature.

The combination of pre-existing authority figures and corporate cultures that exert pressure to conform, coupled with our natural desire to belong, puts us at extreme risk of exiling our conscience when we enter our workplaces. Every job is different, with varying challenges, but we are each surrounded with choices we can make to lead or be led.

If you think about it, you can probably come up with several personal examples in your own job where you have allowed yourself to step out of your Christian belief system into an existing framework opposed to your core values. Consider your answers to the following questions:

- Have you ever said, "That's *their* job," as an excuse not to lend a helping hand?
- Do you participate in gossip or slander concerning fellow employees?
- Do you approach associates at work with an attitude of what they can do for you, instead of what you can do for them?
- Do you try to stay under the radar just to get by?
- Do you measure your personal success through raises, bonuses, promotions, titles, or awards?

How you answer the questions above helps define how others presently view your personal influence and leadership potential at work. Your actions betray your most dominant values and beliefs to those around you. Therefore, it's important to be aware of what you're communicating about your underlying motivations as you interact with others. Are you acting out of faith-based or self-defined motivations? Do you endorse existing flaws in the culture or model different choices?

The point is that proactively fortifying the internal beliefs and values that naturally give rise to positive behaviors as a reflection of your faith is the path to opening your faith-based potential at work. Lasting direction is not found by seeking to directly address your behaviors or habits. Instead, you have to go one step deeper to build sustainable resolve. If the values are good, the response will also be good.

> Romans 8:28.
> And we know that in all things God works for the good of those who love him, who have been called according to his purpose.

Good leaders know that painting a good vision of success and establishing clear objectives, meaningful rewards, and shared trust are imperative to motivating the team to move forward in a coordinated manner. As Christians we need to remember that our overall vision of success subjugates our job to our life's purpose.

> Colossians 3:23–24. Whatever you do, work at it with all your heart, as working for the Lord, not for men, since you know that you will receive an inheritance from the Lord as a reward. It is the Lord Christ you are serving.

The most admired leaders receive our respect because they are comfortable acting on their own internally grounded motivations and resolve. We are drawn to them because they provide an answer we can embrace that supersedes competing choices.

The key to tapping the same energy that fuels exemplary leaders is to realize that our faith should not only coexist with our career, but it should *lead* our career.

Don't worry if you do not like the limelight. You're not being asked to take the television pulpit and become the next Billy Graham! You only need to keep your faith alive within you while at work, so that it is consistently evidenced by your actions.

As Christians, our careers are intended to be aligned with our life's purpose of glorifying God's majesty and helping others receive his gift of grace by accepting Jesus Christ as Lord and Savior. Work simply represents one of our personal spheres of contact and influence where we can let God's love show through us. The next time you're asked to define your optimal work/life balance, simply reply, "One hundred percent life!" Work is a subordinate consideration that should never be allowed the power to challenge your faith-inspired direction in life. By keeping this perspective constantly alive, we will remain in sync with God's plan in all we do.

Think of the additional opportunities this creates for us to achieve our calling! Every sales call, every team meeting, and all our corporate e-mails are additional milestones toward the completion of our life's overall purpose.

New jobs, eventual retirement, family dinner, community service—everything is held together with a single thread. When we start each day with a pre-decided choice to seek our inspiration from what we know to be truly lasting, we simplify what can otherwise seem overwhelming.

The bottom line is that our continued engagement in God's overall plan matters. This is true whether we are at home or at work. How we lead as Christians, regardless of our role or level in an organization, can dramatically impact others.

Faith First, Work Second

Take stock of the role work plays in your life. What compromises do you currently make at work that you know to be in conflict with Christian values or beliefs?

If you know your starting point, you can gauge your progress in finding your motivation and resolve in your faith, not in your job.

Go to study session:
#2. Faith Applies to All We Do, page 73.

It all begins with having faith.

Part I
Finding Inspiration

Have faith.

I

It Starts With Faith

If we are going to let faith inspire our behaviors at work, we first have to have a solid understanding of what our faith entails. Fortunately, the Bible provides a very straightforward definition of faith:

> Hebrews 11:1.
> Now faith is being sure of what we hope for and certain of what we do not see.

When we have faith in God's Word, it becomes the basis of our value and belief system and the source of the inspiration behind our actions. We learn to turn to Scripture, counsel, and prayer to help us maneuver through uncharted territory, and we cease to be molded by popular opinions or practices that are in conflict with what we know to be the truth.

> 1 Peter 1:8–9.
> Though you have not seen him, you love him; and even though you do not see him now, you believe in him and are filled with an inexpressible and glorious joy, for you are receiving the goal of your faith, the salvation of your souls.

Though we don't see him, we know Jesus is always present and ready to guide any decision. And although our hope of salvation lies in the future, it is within reach and is more lasting than the time that has already lapsed.

Because of its boundless potential, faith is intended to be the foundation that supports our entire lives, not just occasions when we find it easiest to apply, such as periodically at home or anonymously in our congregations on Sunday. Expressing our appreciation for it at those times is essential, but we never fully develop as Christians until we leverage its true strength.

> Luke 6:47–48.
> As for everyone who comes to me and hears my words and puts them into practice, I will show you what they are like. They are like a man building a house, who dug down deep and laid the foundation on rock....

Real faith is something that provides the foundation for our life, every aspect of it. Faith doesn't just have a place in our life; it is more appropriate to say that our life has a place in our faith—that everything we do has a role in contributing to the greater sense of purpose.

Most people first find their faith through family members, established friendships, religious institutions, or personal experience. That is why we find it easiest to express our religious beliefs in comparable circumstances. It is normal that we find comfort in what and who we already know.

We are less likely to discover or share our faith at work. That is why we also find it difficult to put work and faith into a shared context. As a result of this separation, our sense of purpose at work risks becoming molded by values encountered through our jobs, versus our time at work being guided by our constant purpose.

Time spent at work is most often time spent cut off from our Christian support structures, as we are imbedded in an environment that teems with conflicting doctrines and values. Accordingly, we routinely face extraneous pressures that seek to derail any ingoing resolve to rely on our faith as the basis for all aspects of our lives.

One way or another we will make choices while doing our job; that is unavoidable. The question is whether our choices will be guided by our Christian values, or will we let arbitrary forces shape our direction.

John F. Kennedy, in his Pulitzer Prize-winning *Profiles in Courage,* illustrated how several politicians were able to remain true to their internal ideals when confronted with intense pressure to compromise the dictates of their consciences. Written in 1955 while Kennedy was a junior senator from Massachusetts, he succinctly provided examples of how respected senators from the annals of American history had persevered in their commitment to unpopular principles, despite being constantly buffeted by the desire to be liked by fellow politicians, to be re-elected back home, or to ameliorate pressures from powerful constituents.

John Quincy Adams was one of the senators highlighted in *Profiles in*

Courage. His political decisions were strongly guided by his allegiance to the same Puritan principles of his father, John Adams, second president of the United Sates, who said, "The magistrate is the servant not of his own desires, not even of the people, but of his God." Because of this belief, John Quincy Adams supported the Embargo Bill of 1807 that sought to punish England for the practice of boarding American sailing vessels and pressing American sailors into service on British warships. In retrospect, the choice appears righteous and patriotic, but for John Quincy Adams it meant opposing the appeasement policies of his own political party and endorsing trade restrictions that would prove to be ruinous to the commercial interests of his home state of Massachusetts. Notwithstanding the ramifications, he chose to act in accordance with his deeply held beliefs and played a key role in getting the bill turned into law. As a result he was socially ostracized and forced to resign his senate seat—all because he put what he believed to be the greater good ahead of more partisan interests.

John Quincy Adams would rebound from his political exile to become the sixth president of the United States and also once again represent Massachusetts, this time as a congressman. But it is not the achievements of the senators celebrated in *Profiles in Courage* that are of interest. It is the fact they all held on to dominant beliefs and values to fortify their resolve so they could weather the external pressures that assailed them. They led from the inside out.

The act of resisting the natural inclination to fall in line with dominant public opinion or party doctrine also has corollaries in today's highly publicized political arena. Thankfully, not all jobs or choices risk the same potential for public flogging, but the firestorms that surround most controversial political stances do provide great examples of the forces that exist in all of our jobs.

This topic resonates with me because I can plainly see the flaws in my past attempts to maintain separation between what I wanted to achieve professionally and what God intended for me personally. Because the two paths were often in conflict, I continually adjusted my work/life balance equation, erroneously allowing my professional aspirations to capture a larger portion of my focus. As a result, I often sought different sources of motivation than the internal ones maintained by the senators profiled in John F. Kennedy's book.

Over time I learned to practice being a good Christian at home and in the community, but I still spent most of my time at work. There, I mostly relied on basic concepts of right and wrong to place expansive guardrails around my activities. My Christian values—"Live by the Golden Rule," "Obey the Ten Commandments," etc.—became more of a moral speed bump for me once I shifted into work mode. I did not rely on my faith as my *inspiration* for my activities. As a result, I eventually felt that the spiritual growth I was cultivating at home hit a wall when I walked into the office.

What's worse, I only came to the realization in recent years that over time, I had let values and beliefs encountered in my professional life reshape my internal guidance system, even though many of the new beliefs were in direct conflict with the truth I would have found in Scripture, had I stayed close to the source.

All of a sudden I found myself equating someone's being "good" with being "saved," and openly rationalizing that "No loving Father would deny any of his children access to his home." In effect, I had rationalized myself out of my part in God's plan.

Additionally, corporate perquisites that included limousines on demand, VIP access to celebrity-studded clubs and events, and evenings spent in five-star hotels and restaurants were readily assimilated into my personal life, as were the late night/early morning parties and the focus on self-aggrandizement. Compromise had become fact as I actively sought to define what was right, based upon my unique experiences and knowledge.

My desire to be friendly toward everyone inadvertently linked the societal influences I encountered with the Christian faith I professed. The two sets of values, which I had tried to keep separate, had blended over time.

My pride in my professional success throughout my career had blurred the big picture, and I had become accustomed to relying on my personal judgment of what was right and wrong to shape my internal compass. Undeniably, work had come to be a source of purpose for me, instead of remaining just one of many avenues for fulfilling my real purpose.

In the end, my religion was just that—*my own custom religion* that supported my professional goals and justified the lifestyle I wanted to live. Thankfully, God has since put people in my life who have helped me regain his desired focus for my future—surrendering came hard, but better late than never!

I've since learned from others to appreciate that my experience is far from unique. Pressure to conform exists in every job. And when the pressure to adopt conflicting ideals comes from people we genuinely respect or enjoy, we find it even more challenging not to stray from the course we have set for ourselves as Christians. Instead, we make compromises, choosing to take detours and placing our hope on getting to the same destination as originally planned, just over longer, bumpier stretches of road. However, all the time we do so, we know in our hearts that we are creating a void between these new routes and our desired destination that we cannot fill. We've replaced certainty with guesswork, so our detours end up leading to dead ends.

In our worst cases, we even take on the role of becoming evangelists who seek new converts to propagate our own mistakes. I know I've certainly done my share of teaching others to adopt the arbitrary worlds found in different companies. One day I'd be assimilating into the culture of a new company; the next day I'd find myself zealously bringing others into the fold.

It all began when I first chose to let outside forces provide the impetus that moved me forward; instead of relying on a strong faith as my source of motivation. In comparison, it is clear that real wisdom comes with maintaining principles of faith as permanent sources of inspiration, whether at home or at work.

I'm still a very firm proponent of creating unique, cohesive corporate identities and a big believer in fostering meritocracies at work, but the source of my personal motivation has changed. I now find much less fuel for my drive in what external values dictate and more in what my faith inspires. The peace I experience because of this change is undeniable, and therein lies an essential premise: "*We should always rely on our faith to guide our work, not let our work guide our faith.*" This mirrors Paul's exhortation to the Romans.

> Romans 12:2.
> Don't copy the behavior and customs of this world, but let God transform you into a new person by changing the way you think. Then you will learn to know God's will for you, which is good and pleasing and perfect.
> —NLT

When we take on the mantle of a Christian, we become a new person, one who has moved his or her allegiance from the ways of the world to the will of God. In doing so, we begin to readily rely on his counsel for all situations and become internally driven toward our goals in a manner congruent with our faith.

Note that humility is a vital component to building our faith. Accepting God's will requires being humble and accepting that his purpose for our life is better than any of our own design.

Believing in our own, self-defined description of what it means to be a good Christian is tantamount to belief in ourselves, not belief in God. As I've noted above, I am guilty of having gone this route for most of my life. Part of my fault was not recognizing (or accepting) the difference between restlessly seeking spiritual fulfillment and fully embracing Christianity as my path to fulfillment.

We can be "spiritual" and piece together religious thought or viewpoints from various sources, but being a Christian implies complete reliance on the teachings of Jesus Christ. The prior route assumes that we, despite our inherent faults and spiritual immaturity, have the flawless ability to discern the truth, based upon our own intellect, while the latter route requires submitting to the fact that God knows more than we do and has made his will known to us in Scripture.

The relevant analogy we regularly hear is that of children and their parents. It is a sound example.

Parents show their love for their children by striving to teach them beliefs and values to live by, so the children can make wise choices and be happy. Parents also provide boundaries that are meant to protect children from avoidable harm or distress. Yet it is the nature of children of every age to challenge the rules and boundaries around them in an effort to fulfill their individual desires for selfish expression, exploration, and control.

It is not easy for children to wholly submit to the will of their parents. As a result, kids often do things that then result in undesirable consequences, which could have been avoided had they taken their parents' advice—like the time I ignored my dad's warning and grabbed a hornet's nest, thinking I could get some honey; not a good idea!

Negative outcomes are even more likely if the parents fail to provide good guidance in the first place—something that is unavoidable, as none of us is perfect.

Because we soon discover our parents don't have all the answers, we feel empowered to explore new options. As we grow up and our worlds expand, we find we have greater and greater flexibility to either accept or create new guidelines by which to live our lives. Invariably we adopt new rules and establish new boundaries that we then attempt to pass on to the next generation, and the process continues, as they in turn test our beliefs and evolve new rules for governing their lives.

This innate resistance to humbling ourselves and putting unconditional faith in a higher power continues throughout our lives, even long after we achieve independence from our childhood households—except the struggle then becomes focused between the will of our heavenly Father and us, as his children.

The major difference here is that unlike that of our earthly parents or guardians, his will and his plans are perfect. They define the ultimate truth and purpose for our lives and provide fixed boundaries of right and wrong. These, in turn, are constant and predictable. They do not evolve from generation to generation based upon societal influences, nor do they suffer from human error. Still, just like a three-year-old who wants his honey, we continually resist submitting to the guidance of a benevolent, loving father.

A starting point for letting faith to be our inspiration for our actions is to first come to the conclusion that we are ready to wholeheartedly put our trust in God's Word and unconditionally accept his will as the guiding force in our life.

Show humility. Stop seeking to make his truths fit into your perception of reality, and humbly acknowledge that you don't know the whole picture. In so doing, you'll find your trust in God's plan is well founded. It is nice to have a dependable source of strength from which to draw inspiration, especially while at work, when you find yourself cut off from your normal support structures. The alternative is to allow yourself to be shaped by random forces that are also beyond your control. It is your choice to which you will submit.

Submission does not mean we are expected to put aside the conscious pursuit of new things in our life. It is still good practice to prayerfully make requests of God that reflect our heartfelt concerns and needs, but in the end, it is the discipline of unconditionally accepting God's decision that leads to contentment instead of disappointment.

Those of us who are parents sometimes allow our children to do things that we know are not in their best interests. We either get worn down by their repeated requests, or we just make flawed decisions. But it is against God's nature to make similar mistakes, so we are best served by accepting his plan for us, whatever that might be.

Don't feel this means he is not listening or not giving thought to our requests. Even Jesus made requests of God that were not filled. But Jesus also placed his faith in God's ultimate decision. Consider his plea made in the garden of Gethsemane when faced with his impending crucifixion:

Matthew 26:39.
Going a little farther, he fell with his face to the ground and prayed, "My Father, if it is possible, may this cup be taken from me. Yet not as I will, but as you will."

Jesus shows he experienced trepidation concerning the end he faced, but he never questioned whether God's plan was right; rather, he knew that in the end he would do as God willed. Similarly, by accepting Jesus Christ as our Lord and Savior and opening our hearts so God can work through us, we become willing participants in God's plan. We just have to remember that this applies twenty-four hours a day, seven days a week, including our time at work.

Faith Check

State a faith-based objective for your life that your work needs to support. Choose to define how work fits your personal goals, rather than letting work arbitrarily pick the path for you.

Go to study session:
#3. On Faith and Submission to God's Will, page 78.

II

Share the Love

Unconditionally loving others is the ultimate expression of being a Christian. As such, it should be reflected in all of our interactions.

> Matthew 22:37–40.
> Jesus replied: "Love the Lord your God with all your heart and with all your soul and with all your mind." This is the first and greatest commandment. And the second is like it: "Love your neighbor as yourself." All the Law and the Prophets hang on these two commandments.

Love is fundamental to living a Christian life. In fact, the word "love" is mentioned 610 times in the Bible—289 times in the New Testament alone. Therefore, it follows that love also needs to be central to one's Christian-faith-based leadership qualities at work, which is why you'll notice it commands so much attention throughout this book.

If you have ever been to a Christian wedding, chances are very good that you heard the following definition of love from the Bible:

> 1 Corinthians 13:4–7.
> Love is patient, love is kind. It does not envy, it does not boast, it is not proud. It is not rude, it is not self-seeking, it is not easily angered, it keeps no record of wrongs. Love does not delight in evil but rejoices with the truth. It always protects, always trusts, always hopes, always perseveres.

It is a great passage, one that resonates well with the soon-to-be newlywed couple that has reached the crossroads of joining each other in true partnership. But it should be kept in mind that the Bible is not merely exhorting us to love our betrothed. It is a calling to all Christians to daily live our lives as an expression of love.

Many of us find it easy to show love to friends and family, even to strangers. But then we tone it down at work. After all, many of us feel "work is not personal"—wrong! Considering the number of interactions we have during our work lives, work actually presents one of our largest opportunities for personal impact and growth.

Standing by each other and taking advantage of every opportunity we have to share our love is part of God's plan for us to experience a fulfilling life. Recognize that love is intended to be the underlying motivation for all of our actions; he is not asking us to just tolerate or simply help others. Without a basis in love, good deeds are just good deeds and not a reflection of our faith in God's Word.

> 1 Corinthians 13:1–3.
> If I speak in the tongues of men and of angels, but have not love, I am only a resounding gong or a clanging cymbal. If I have the gift of prophecy and can fathom all mysteries and all knowledge, and if I have a faith that can move mountains, but have not love, I am nothing. If I give all I possess to the poor and surrender my body to the flames, but have not love, I gain nothing.

This is why love is best thought of as an action verb, not merely an aspirational state or feeling. It is the true representation of our faith, because ultimately, all of our behaviors reflect our real beliefs and values.

Assume you are lying in bed at night, and you believe your house is on fire. What action would you take? Would you go back to sleep and hope it passes? Or would you be motivated by your belief in the fire and the values you hold dear to take a more proactive course of action, like rousing your family or friends and getting out of harm's way?

Now, reflect on what it means to really believe in God's Word and Jesus Christ as Lord and Savior. Do your actions reflect that belief, or are you at odds with other doctrines and views that are struggling inside you for control of your motivations? Are you going back to sleep or proactively acting on your faith?

Putting our Christian faith into daily expression requires conscious commitment. It takes a lot of effort to regularly evaluate our actions toward others with a subjective eye, making a personal assessment of our underlying motives and striving to keep our behaviors aligned with our love for others.

Even though we can all accept love as a positive virtue, we also know it is not easy to always express ourselves in a loving manner. It is hard, as humans, not to let selfish motives enter into our expectations. We are also prone to letting our own perceptions or flaws impair our ability to fully love everyone. Despite these challenges, faith leads us to experience joy through fulfilling the desire to raise up someone else, with no regard for what we may receive in return. This requires a willingness to lovingly plant and patiently nurture the positive seeds of our faith in order for them to grow and benefit others.

Consider what Jesus endured at the moment of his crucifixion as the result of his loving the world. Talk about being underappreciated! If we also look past the present and keep our thoughts on the hope and promise of what our faith means for our future, we won't be disappointed.

> 1 Peter 3:8–9.
> Finally, all of you, live in harmony with one another; be sympathetic, love as brothers, be compassionate and humble. Do not repay evil with evil or insult with insult, but with blessing, because to this you were called so that you may inherit a blessing.

As we elevate our awareness of our motives, we will note that when our actions are born out of the love, inspired by our faith, they will be positive in nature. We can't go wrong when we share the love.

Love for All

Caring for the people with whom we interact as part of our professional activities—subordinates, bosses, or peers; Millennials, Gen-Xers, Baby Boomers, or Traditionalists; Christians, Muslims, Buddhists, or atheists; company employees or external contacts—is a positive act that will result in a more positive work environment and greater personal fulfillment. When it comes to sharing the love, all are deserving of our gift.

> Romans 2:11.
> For God does not show favoritism.

Truly, God sent Jesus to save us all.

John 3:16.
For God so loved the world that he gave his one and only
Son, that whoever believes in him shall not perish but have
eternal life.

Because of the all-inclusive nature of the underlying invitation, John
3:16 is arguably the most memorized and widely evangelized Christian
Scripture in the Bible. If you watch sporting events on TV you have
probably seen it proclaimed on a sign held by somebody in a rainbow-
colored hairdo or possibly in the eye-black on the cheeks of Tim Tebow
as he quarterbacked the Florida Gators to the NCAA National Football
title in 2009.

Although seeing the open invitation of John 3:16 is encouraging for
all, living it is the charge of being someone who has already professed his
or her faith in the path to enjoying eternal life. The power of our faith is
measured by the impact it has on others.

The Goal Is to Share God's Love, Not to Perform Good Deeds

We can perform good deeds for someone without loving him or her.
Conversely, if we start with love and act in a loving manner, our deeds will
be inherently good. For example, we cannot outwardly convey our faith
through love, yet break any of the Ten Commandments. Think about it.

The relevant distinction is that the performance of good acts is not the
process for gaining redemption. In and of themselves, acts that are not an
outpouring of our faith have no redeeming value.

Galatians 2:16.
Know that a man is not justified by observing the law, but by
faith in Jesus Christ. So we, too, have put our faith in Christ
Jesus that we may be justified by faith in Christ and not by
observing the law, because by observing the law no one will
be justified.

In other words, we can't earn our way into heaven by following the
Ten Commandments, or by donating large sums of money to charity, or
by serving in soup kitchens if we are not doing so as an expression of our
faith. The emphasis is first on believing and then on doing.

Good acts are the natural result of our accepting and sharing God's
love, which we can't earn because he freely gives it to all who are faithful.

And the faithful, in turn, share that love because they are motivated to do so by their dominant beliefs and values. In this way, faith gives rise to positive actions that are the outward beacons for others to find the outpouring of God's love through his servant leaders.

Share His Love

Your ability to love unconditionally is a measure of your real belief in Christ's teachings. Sharing God's love with others keeps you close to him. He is why we love.

Start each day identifying an opportunity for you to put someone else's needs above your own. End each day evaluating how successful you've been at doing so.

Go to study sessions:
#4. All with Love, page 84.
#5. Faith Trumps Law, page 88.

III

All Christians Are Leaders

As Christians, we are meant to be conduits for God's love, to let it flow through us to those around us, not to simply bask in the light of the truth for our own fulfillment.

> Matthew 5:14–16.
> You are the light of the world. A city on a hill cannot be hidden. Neither do people light a lamp and put it under a bowl. Instead they put it on its stand, and it gives light to everyone in the house. In the same way, let your light shine before men, that they may see your good deeds and praise your Father in heaven.

These verses state it plainly: If you are a light, it is your character to shine. And if you have a light, let it shine. Why snuff it out and sit in darkness when you don't have to?

The source of your light is found in the faith that glows inside you. By remaining true to that source of inspiration, you allow its light to be seen outwardly through your actions. The key is realizing that you have been given a gift that is intended to be shared. You are called to let your faith lead you in all you do so that others may also come to appreciate, know, and praise the glory of God.

The continual desire to save more people through expression of the love that wells up because of one's faith is a basic theme throughout the New Testament. It was evident when Jesus dined with tax collectors and when he told the parable of the shepherd who leaves his flock to seek his one lost sheep. It was also a driving force behind the preaching of the apostles, compelling Paul to make his broad, sweeping journeys to extend God's promise to the Gentiles. Such was their love for others that they continually shared it through words and actions with everyone they could reach at a time when they were seen as an outcast minority.

Conversely, denial, hoarding, and inaction constitute hindrances to spiritual growth. They stunt personal growth and also keep God's love from reaching others. In effect, this is what we do whenever we keep love dormant.

This is one of the lessons found in Matthew 25:14–30, in the parable of the three servants left to watch over their master's property while he went on a journey. In the end, the servant who hid his allotment to protect it had it taken away by the master and given to one who invested his portion wisely. Moral of the story: Those who take what they are given and effectively employ it on behalf of their master will get more. Those who fail to wisely employ what they are given will lose all.

When taken in the context of our job, the goal is to maintain the internal motivation to invest God's love through our actions toward everyone with whom we interact. By doing so, we will find it both liberating and rewarding, as the whole of our life becomes reflective of the faith that guides us.

This may feel counterintuitive if we presently have challenging situations or personalities to deal with at work. I know it was hard for me to finally flip the switch and look past my differences with others regarding motivation, objective, or style. How could serving the interests of someone I suspect may be acting out of selfish interest or misguided beliefs be a positive output of my faith?

For me, these situations boiled down to accepting that I could not control or fully comprehend the other person's underlying intentions. I could only choose to follow my own internal counsel or to disregard it and revert to my historical (i.e., wrong) solution, which was to let the external situation guide my response.

What I've found is that when I rest my decision on where my faith leads me, I come away with both a sense of remaining on stride to meet my larger goal in life and an overriding sense of peace, knowing I can trust that in the end, everything will be as God intends.

This doesn't mean my day job is always smooth sailing. Far from it! Conflicts still abound in my professional interactions, and I'm confident they will continue to exist for all of us as long as we remain a collection of unique individuals.

Additionally, loving others does not necessitate complete acquiescence to the requests or choices of those around us. We are still expected to utilize the intellect and talents we've been given to contribute to the greater good of the collective team (remember the parable of the three servants?). Doing so will naturally lead to disagreements and conflicts. The challenge is to be sure we facilitate positive conflict that takes the team and organization to a better solution. Checking in with our faith will help ensure that outcome.

Belief Starts inside You

Part of being a Christian is the inherent belief that we've been asked to consciously take the love of God through Jesus to heart. From that internal well, we can draw the inspiration to share God's love through our actions.

Luke 6:45.

The good man brings good things out of the good stored up in his heart, and the evil man brings evil things out of the evil stored up in his heart. For out of the overflow of his heart his mouth speaks.

Brings is the operative word; thus, the calling to *be* a Christian. Our life's endeavor is not merely to study and know what a Christian is or how one is supposed to act. Study and reflection definitely help cement our belief, but then we are charged with letting that belief express itself according to its nature.

James 2:19, 26.

You believe that there is one God. Good! Even the demons believe that—and shudder …[26]As the body without the spirit is dead, so faith without deeds is dead.

As the saying goes, the proof of the pudding is in the eating. Likewise, the proof of our faith is found in the positive intentions of our actions. It begins with seeking the truth and establishing a relationship with God through acceptance of his grace by believing in Jesus as our Lord and Savior. Once found, our relationship with God will naturally give rise to acts that reflect our faith. Overall, the development process still has to have its beginning in us, and in the end, it has to be expressed through us.

Regardless of our profession, we all have the opportunity to choose to act on our faith. To illustrate: because I mostly worked in supermarkets and restaurants growing up, I still love to see workers in the best of those venues selflessly step out of their individual roles to help their colleagues. In a supermarket, the situation may be that a checker is falling behind ringing up groceries, and I'll see someone step in to help bag groceries, or another checker may delay taking his or her break or come off break early to help ease the demand. In a restaurant, it may involve seeing the day shift cleaning and prepping items for the night crew during downtime, instead of relaxing and taking extended breaks.

Similar examples of selfless behaviors can be readily given for construction, farming, or any other job. The point is we are all afforded the opportunity to find positive motivation in the tenets and principles of our faith. It just takes the willingness to let it out to see it in action.

In order to put our faith into action, it is also vital that we put aside any reservations about our being qualified to represent Christianity. Any time we act in accordance with our faith, we are doing well by our religion. Don't let fears of doing the wrong thing keep you from doing the right thing.

Even Paul had his challenges, but they did not impede his commitment to his new life.

> John 7:21–25.
> So I find this law at work: Although I want to do good, evil is right there with me. For in my inner being I delight in God's law; but I see another law at work in me, waging war against the law of my mind and making me a prisoner of the law of sin at work within me. What a wretched man I am! Who will rescue me from this body that is subject to death? Thanks be to God, who delivers me through Jesus Christ our Lord! ...

To err is human. Don't confuse being unavoidably flawed with being a hypocrite. A hypocrite is someone who purposely presents a false façade that is not representative of his or her true intentions. That is far removed from consciously seeking to find positive motivation in the loving nature of our faith and coming up short. Our built-in imperfection is part of the plan.

Romans 11:32.
For God has bound everyone over to disobedience so that he
may have mercy on them all.

View shortcomings in knowledge or action as areas for continued study
and prayer. Failing forward is a good goal.

How widely your efforts will actually be appreciated, reinforced, or
emulated at work will partly depend on your work environment's current
culture and the dominant values held by the people you encounter. It
would be naïve to assume that everyone at work will positively respond to
your taking an unselfish approach to conducting yourself. Some may even
think you are being insincere or harboring ulterior motives. Keep focused
on your ultimate goal and take heart. Even Christ's closest followers
experienced moments of doubt until additional events made believers out
of them.

As with any cultural change, it will take consistency over time for
positive momentum to build from our actions; we may never personally
observe our full impact. Once we have faith, however, there is no choice
but to move forward.

John 13:17.
Now that you know these things, you will be blessed if you
do them.

The opportunities to share the love are endless, but sometimes they also
require trying something new. As an example, you may work in a company
that is arranged in various functions, such as operations, finance, and sales,
which need to work well together to grow the business. A major challenge
in this type of matrix organization is to ensure that a shared vision of
success and communal values permeates the entire organization. This is
needed to instill a cohesive sense of purpose that will keep company-wide
objectives at the forefront of everyone's priorities. When this is achieved,
the result is high-performing organizations with well-formed avenues of
communication and cooperation. When this is not fully achieved, there
will be varying degrees of dysfunctional motivations and behavior that
lead to sub-optimal decisions.

Just like children, functions seem to have a natural tendency to seek
complete autonomy. And as functional identities become incongruent
with a unified corporate vision, functional goals also become more and

more self-contained, reinforcing barriers that discourage cross-functional partnership.

This is not to say that functional goals and values are bad, in and of themselves. They are actually very desirable to give close-in guidance to functional team members. It is when they are not aligned with a broader corporate vision that they create issues.

In such situations, I've seen divergent priorities and conflicting values among the functions begin to give rise to widespread distrust of underlying agendas and a lack of shared commitment across the organization. As a result, individuals naturally retreat into their respective areas of accountability, where the world is less murky, opting to focus on their own tasks and minimizing the cross-functional cooperation that is intended to be the strength of the matrix organization.

Maybe you can relate to some of the following examples, where in lieu of a common goal, functional silos have accomplished their internal objectives but have negatively impacted total company results:

- The marketing department's developing programming that is highly creative but too complex to implement
- The sales team's securing customer commitments that hit volume targets but have negative impact on profits
- Operations groups enacting cost-cutting measures that improve margins but inadvertently reduce competitive differentiation of products, leading to competitive inroads and lower sales volumes
- Everyone's finding selfish opportunities to spend their entire budget, even when they know better uses for some of their funds exists elsewhere in the company.

In each of the above instances, decisions could have been improved through effective cross-functional partnering and collaboration. Although the functions achieved their respective mandates, low commitment to shared goals and low value placed on unselfish cooperation between functions led to wasted resources and undesirable outcomes. Further, because the negative impact of these self-centered actions was measurable, the source of each problem eventually got on senior management's radar, and actions were taken to completely revamp processes and personnel in the self-serving departments. Thus, hiding behind the walls of the functional silo was for naught. The stronger the walls were built around each silo, the more the pressure built to break down the walls and the more forceful the action taken when the walls came down.

Regardless of your chosen profession, the lesson is the same: no matter how fragmented your work environment, it should not impact your choice to assert your positive intentions to help create positive change. It comes back to letting your faith guide your work, not to letting your work guide your faith.

Breaking down barriers between departments is definitely one of the more difficult—and fulfilling—challenges I've regularly embraced throughout my career. As a result, I can testify that disparate functional silos are a real issue that can be readily be found in varying degrees of immobility in most organizations. However, in all cases, I can attest that the overwhelming majority of employees recognize the negative implications of propagating the isolationistic tendencies of rigid functional silos. Thus, they willingly gravitate toward positive change that leads to a more supportive team atmosphere; one grounded in mutual respect, trust, and love of one another. In effect, they are drawn to what God offers.

That is where you come in. You have a positive beginning in your faith that desires expression in order to achieve fulfillment. Don't let your time spent at work become a void that impedes your spiritual growth. Perhaps your sphere of influence is as simple as providing a smile to someone or changing the tone of your e-mails to another person. Everything counts. Remember your real purpose, and let the spirit guide you to reach others through all that you do. The good news is that people are looking for what you have to offer!

Fear not; you can only do well by your associates at work if you are being led in the real spirit of the truth. Do you really think someone will complain that you have put the good of the team ahead of your own agenda?

Little Beginnings Can Have Great Impact on People's Lives

Regardless of the breadth of our role at work, we all have the opportunity to have a positive impact that will resonate throughout the organization.

Galatians 5:9.
A little yeast works through the whole batch of dough.

No contribution is too small. Every small act of kindness and sincerity can have a lasting effect. You may have heard this concept described in secular circles as "paying it forward," or "the ripple effect." It captures the very nature of how Christianity has grown to be the largest religion in the world today and why the Bible still remains the most published book of all time. It is also the manner in which the Kingdom of God is coming to fruition.

> Mark 4:30–32.
> Again he said, "What shall we say the kingdom of God is like, or what parable shall we use to describe it? It is like a mustard seed, which is the smallest seed you plant in the ground. Yet when planted, it grows and becomes the largest of all garden plants, with such big branches that the birds of the air can perch in its shade."

The parable of the miniscule mustard seed's giving rise to a great shrub is a great representation of how faith can blossom in us individually and how we can, in turn, generate future growth for others, building up the one great tree that is the overall community of God.

With this in mind, we must also remember not to blindly fall victim to assuming that Christianity itself is something that attained full bloom in ancient times. In actuality, it has not yet come to maturity. It remains our collective responsibility as individual Christians to continue fueling its growth. How we bring God's love to work is just another avenue for us to allow the truth to prosper.

Almost everyone has a story about the effect one person or several people had in shaping their lives through a simple act or statement. Sometimes these are aspirational examples, and other times they are negative; both show our actions matter.

I distinctly remember several people who had a positive impact on the choices and actions I've taken throughout my life. I can also draw one similarity across all of them that might ring true with your own memories. Whether they were parents, teachers, coworkers, pastors, strangers, or friends, they all had one thing in common: they genuinely cared and wanted the best for me.

That is the power of true Christian love—the power to influence others in a positive manner. May we all find the faith that gives rise to such love! Certainly it is the very blessing Paul sought for Christ's followers in his letter to the church at Ephesus, and as such, it provides a great close to Part I of this book.

Ephesians 3:16–21.

I pray that out of his glorious riches he may strengthen you with power through his Spirit in your inner being, so that Christ may dwell in your hearts through faith. And I pray that you, being rooted and established in love, may have power, together with all the saints, to grasp how wide and long and high and deep is the love of Christ, and to know this love that surpasses knowledge—that you may be filled to the measure of all the fullness of God.

Now to him who is able to do immeasurably more than all we ask or imagine, according to his power that is at work within us, to him be glory in the church and in Christ Jesus throughout all generations, for ever and ever! Amen.

Lead On

Leading is the natural result of acting, based upon our deeply held beliefs and values. It is something we all do every day; we all influence each other. By consistently finding our motivation and resolve in the principles of our faith, we lead in the direction intended.

How can your actions at work better reflect your faith?

Go to study sessions:
#6. All Christians Are Leaders, page 94.
#7. Faith Is an Active State, page 98.

Part II

Inspired Behavior

Together we fulfill our purpose.

IV

The Servant Leader

The speed and complexity of today's world makes us appreciate quick fixes and shortcuts in order to be more efficient. From a leadership perspective, this has given rise to numerous books on how effective leaders operate, because we appreciate what they do. By reading about the actions of admired leaders, our hope is that we will have the same success if we emulate their externally exhibited habits and characteristics.

We are comfortable with behavior-based self-help books, because they deal with subject matter we can visualize and measure, which gives us a means to outwardly evaluate our own success at mimicking desirable traits. But in truth, without the same internal values and beliefs that fuel another person's motivations and resolve, the likelihood of consistently applying the leadership skills of that individual to our unique situations is fairly slim. Instead, it is much more likely we will choose to follow the recommendations toward which we are predisposed because they are aligned with our pre-existing motivations.

The real question to understand is not *how* revered leaders led, but *why* they made the choices they did. Their internal drivers are what inevitably gave rise to their external actions.

The next time you have a choice to make, you can answer the question "What would Jesus do?" and you'll make the right choice, but then take the challenging next step and ask, "*Why* would Jesus do that?" Then you will find real insights that will help refine your faith, reinforcing your ability to be a truly inspired leader—that is a key point.

For example, if Jesus was working in a warehouse and he saw someone knock over a stack of product, what would he do? Why would he do it?

Unless we find ourselves in a similar situation, we're not likely to be able to re-enact what Jesus would do, but we can share his internal motivations, which are applicable to choices we have to make during the course of our job.

That is why I have emphasized belief in God's Word and Jesus Christ as Lord and Savior as requisite elements of working with purpose—so that we can share the following internal motivations to fuel our daily interactions at work:

- *Shared purpose* governs our daily lives.
- *Hope* of salvation keeps us pointed in the right direction.
- *Love* that seeks expression is the engine that moves us forward.
- *Leadership* is the result of answering the call to engage our engines and move forward.

Reinforcing our commitment to these components of our faith helps establish a solid foundation on which we can rely for support as we engage in our daily interactions. With these factors as internal influences, we can then better visualize examples of how our Christian faith may outwardly express itself through our personal leadership behavior at work.

To begin with, Christian leadership is best described as *servant leadership*. It is all about the people we seek to benefit, not about embellishing our own stature.

> Luke 22:26.
> But among you it will be different. Those who are the greatest among you should take the lowest rank, and the leader should be like a servant. —NLT

This was amply portrayed by the story of Christ's washing the feet of his disciples, the King of Kings, lowering himself to serve his followers in the most menial of tasks. While doing so, he also exhorted his disciples to take on the posture of serving others.

> Matthew 20:26–28.
> Whoever wants to become great among you must be your servant, and whoever wants to be first must be your slave—just as the Son of Man did not come to be served, but to serve, and to give his life as a ransom for many.

These verses clearly state the mind-set we should have as we go about our daily routines. If we are followers of Christ, then we will naturally do what is exemplary of Christ and seek opportunities to serve others.

This does not mean that those we seek to serve will always readily embrace our good intentions. In the same manner that God freely offers salvation to all, servant leaders actively create opportunities and environments where people can grow and succeed, but it is the individual's responsibility to accept the offer. Whether or not those we seek to serve actually will choose to take full advantage of the opportunities we provide is where their responsibility takes over.

With that in mind, each of us needs to proactively work at creating positive environments where everyone can benefit and thrive. Situational influences not only have the power to bring out the worst in people, but they also give rise to heroes.

If you are a manager of others, then you should recognize that you've been given the added responsibility of generating positive momentum with your staff. After all, if a researcher in a lab coat can motivate people to inflict harm, then it also follows that people in positions of authority can influence people to do well.

Regardless of our position in the company hierarchy, this concept is universal. We all have people we can help to grow. Every time we come in contact with another human being, directly or indirectly, we have the chance to benefit someone else. It all begins with accepting our role as a servant leader.

The Reverend Dr. Martin Luther King Jr. integrated this very point into a sermon he gave two months before his death. He said it well:

> And so Jesus gave us a new norm of greatness. If you want to be important—wonderful. If you want to be recognized—wonderful. If you want to be great—wonderful. But recognize that he who is greatest among you shall be your servant. (Amen) That's a new definition of greatness.

> And this morning, the thing that I like about it: by giving that definition of greatness, it means that everybody can be great, (everybody) because everybody can serve. (Amen.) You don't have to have a college degree to serve. (All right.) You don't have to make your subject and your verb agree to serve. You don't have to know about Plato and Aristotle to serve. You don't have to know Einstein's theory of relativity to serve. You

don't have to know the second theory of thermodynamics in physics to serve. (Amen.) You only need a heart full of grace, (yes, sir, amen) a soul generated by love. (Yes.) And you can be that servant.

—Excerpt from *The Drum Major Instinct,* Dr. Martin Luther King Jr., February 4, 1968

Amen, indeed. We all have it in us to serve. That is the natural outpouring of our faith.

Cultural Implication: Need to Redefine "Success"

Think of the snapshot of our last decade. How does the visual of a world full of servant leaders align with your perception of what the world is actually like? What would you define as the predominant cultural values in our society today?

Some of our societal values are evident in the ongoing, heated debate between the proponents of Darwinian evolution and those of creationism. Others are evident by the top-rated reality shows of the day, where winning can justify any means employed to be the last one standing. And still others can be seen in the evolution of the English language.

Many of the words officially added to the Merriam-Webster dictionary in the last couple years reflect the growing assimilation of the Internet into our lifestyles. These include words like:

> Google verb/gü–gəl/: to use the Google search engine to obtain information about (as a person) on the World Wide Web, and

> Blog noun/blȯg, bläg/: a website that contains an online personal journal with reflections, comments, and often hyperlinks provided by the writer; *also:* the contents of such a site.

We also have new additions to our language that capture our growing need for immediate gratification and shortcuts. Even some common texting abbreviations can now be found in the dictionary. Acronyms such as:

> LOL abbr: laugh out loud; laughing out loud, and

> BFF abbr: best friends forever.

Other recent additions officially speak to our penchant for excess and materialism. Examples of these include:

Ginormous/jī-'nȯr-məs/: extremely large: humongous,

Supersize/sü-pər-,sīz /: to increase considerably the size, amount or extent of, and

Bling/bling/: flashy jewelry worn especially as an indication of wealth; *broadly*: expensive and ostentatious possessions.

These newly minted words reflect our capacity for ever-expanding the boundaries of what is possible, as well as continually raising the bar for what we perceive we need. Technology is the new frontier, and self-actualization and expression are our mantras.

Even though per capita income in the United States *doubled* in less than one generation, going from $19,477 in 1990 to $38,615 in 2007, household saving and charitable contribution rates greatly lagged in growth during the same period. The debate surrounding alternate calculation methods aside, what is clear is that our standard of living in the United States is continually improving, and that it is being used to fuel our insatiable appetite for more stuff.

The technology explosion has provided great information and entertainment value, making ginormous high-definition, flat-screen televisions readily available, and putting GPS into the hands of directionally challenged drivers and hikers everywhere. Walk into any school and you will also find that the latest MP3 players and video cell phones have become commonplace.

Thanks to the rapidly changing environment in technology, we find ourselves constantly upgrading to the latest alternative, while adamantly declaring what was recently highly desirable is now obsolete. Our endless obsession with what's next is a product marketer's dream come true, but as a consumer, it sometimes feels as if it would be wiser to swim back to shore with what we have, rather than swimming farther out into a turbulent sea in search of "more and better."

In addition to accumulating new technology, we have also been actively trading up to more expensive alternatives in many categories over the last twenty years. Custom lattes, designer apparel, exotic foods, and adventurous ingredients all are *de rigueur* in contemporary society. What used to be considered premium quality is now expected. And what was once considered frivolous is now a "must-have."

Although the economic travails of the last few years have put a damper on our conspicuous-consumption behavior, many pundits agree our selfish desire for more is just lying dormant, waiting to resurface as the world economy reboots itself.

The form of our personal indulgence may be different when it returns, but the focus is expected to still be on self. We remain addicted to our stuff and the image it conveys about us, despite this recent break from our buying binge of ostentatious items.

Hopefully, our view of where real success lies will be clearer as our financial health returns. However, regardless of our money situation, we always have the ability to serve. Being given more of anything just opens new opportunities for us to benefit others. We simply need the wisdom to heed the good counsel we've received on how to employ the resources we have been entrusted to administer.

> 1 Timothy 6:17–19.
> Command those who are rich in this present world not to be arrogant nor to put their hope in wealth, which is so uncertain, but to put their hope in God, who richly provides us with everything for our enjoyment. Command them to do good, to be rich in good deeds, and to be generous and willing to share. In this way they will lay up treasure for themselves as a firm foundation for the coming age, so that they may take hold of the life that is truly life.

The Bible repeatedly makes it clear that the accumulation of riches can make it harder to gain salvation but not impossible. The difficulty arises when our primary goal or the arbitrary measure we use to gauge our personal success becomes obtaining more worldly riches. When cars, houses, gadgets, rewards, and extravagances become the driving motivation for our work, we lose sight of the larger picture—that everything comes from one source and serves one purpose.

Considering that 33 percent of the world's population (that's approximately *2.2 billion* people!) live at or below the poverty level in their respective countries, it's important to ask ourselves if we really need more than we currently have in order to live a good life. How much of our not being happy with what we *do* have is directly related to our chasing more of what we *do not* have, instead of placing our faith in the greatest gift, which is readily available to us for free?

When we let our faith lead us, we find ways to utilize our resources—not only our money, but also our time, skills, and energy to better the lives of others. When fully embraced, building for personal gain becomes nonexistent because we accept that we have all we need. We entrust God with taking care of tomorrow and appreciate what he has given us today.

Easier said than done. Perhaps you have attained a position, amassed a comfortable lifestyle, or rest your pride on the results of your hard work. Do you find your natural inclination is to consolidate gains while still seeking more? Do you ever fear losing what you have? The harder it is to give up what you have, the more likely it is that those items are symbols of something you really value. Allowing yourself to find the most value in the rewards found in your faith provides true stability and removes the fear of loss or failure, because you can't lose what God gives you.

Keeping our sights on our ultimate destination helps us take our work in stride, as part of the overall plan. By embracing the hope of eternal life through Jesus Christ, we clarify our objectives and establish a footing that won't falter with the ups and downs of our financial situation or professional career. We can confidently move forward with each day and know we are getting closer to our goal, regardless of what we encounter. Whatever transgresses, we are still called to serve.

Importantly, serving others does not mean forced sacrifice. To build on Dr. Martin Luther King Jr.'s sermon, we don't have to be paupers to serve.

Serving others, regardless of who we are, is done willingly and joyfully when love is at its core. We can still enjoy raises and promotions at work. It's okay to receive rewards and recognition for our achievements—in fact, they will very likely follow our good leadership. It's when we put attainment of those items ahead of our primary goal of helping others that we stray from our appointed path and invite feelings of being unfulfilled.

Recognize the implication for how we should measure our success at work. If the ultimate goal is to serve God's purpose, then we need to get in the habit of measuring our performance at work against criteria that gauge whether we are on track to achieving that overarching objective. For example:

- Would your fellow workers describe you as a servant leader or something less flattering?

- Do you avoid contributing to office gossip?
- Are you content with the position and pay you have accepted, or does your desire for more consume much of your effort and thoughts at work?
- Do you feel you have improved or lessened your relationship with God through your recent actions at work?

Promotions and raises, awards and titles—those should all be non-considerations when measuring our success. Those may or may not come, as God wills, and hopefully, we are wise in how we make use of their value as we receive them. Our real reward will come at the final judgment. Selfish ambition just detracts us from our goal and can keep us from enjoying the benefits we can find in everyone around us.

James 3:16–17.
For where you have envy and selfish ambition, there you find disorder and every evil practice. [17]But the wisdom that comes from heaven is first of all pure; then peace-loving, considerate, submissive, full of mercy and good fruit, impartial and sincere.

When I was working my first job out of grad school, the above quoted wisdom would have come in handy. I had joined a top-notch company as one of eight newly minted MBAs and couldn't have been happier with the challenge, the culture, and the pay. A year later, I heard through the grapevine that the company had significantly increased its salary offer to the next candidate class in order to be more price-competitive. This meant the new hires were coming on board with higher salaries than those of us who had more tenure and proven performance.

The news that the entire new class was going to leap-frog me in terms of salary did not affect my work ethic, but it did put a temporary damper on my overall enthusiasm. I felt I wasn't being fairly treated, but what had really changed? The specifics of the job and the collegial atmosphere of the organization were still intact, and my pay was actually higher than when I started, thanks to a performance increase. What I had considered a year earlier to be wonderful had actually gotten better, yet I still felt shortchanged. The only difference was that I had begun comparing my situation to an outward measure that had no relevance. I had fallen into the trap of allowing envy and pride to foment discontent. Similar to the negative consequences associated with "trying to keep up with the Joneses,"

I was allowing an emphasis on someone else's trappings to dictate my benchmark for professional achievement.

In retrospect, I can see there is no reason why I couldn't be happy today with the starting salary I had in my first job, even though it is over twenty years later. Things could be much worse!

The challenge is to hold on to hope in the face of prevalent societal influences that constantly seek to diminish our reliance upon God's promise. If faith is leading us, then our personal situation is not the yardstick we use to measure our success; it is our ability to positively reflect God's light so others can find their way to eternal salvation. Recognizing that lasting success only can be attained beyond the short-lived years of our work and our fluctuating financial situations puts our day jobs in perspective.

Cultural Implication: Need to Redefine "Strength"

Effectively serving others requires finding strength in vulnerability. By becoming subordinate to everyone, we allow ourselves to be weak and accepting that God is ultimately in control, because it is through his grace that we are saved in the end. Conversely, the more we fight to maintain individual control to fulfill our flawed desires and wants in the here and now, the more our actions will reflect our negative intentions.

As much as we want to control our own destiny, submission to the higher power remains the requisite starting point. Think of God as our number-one shareholder, if that makes it easier!

> Colossians 3:12–14.
> Therefore, as God's chosen people, holy and dearly loved, clothe yourselves with compassion, kindness, humility, gentleness and patience. Bear with each other and forgive whatever grievances you may have against one another. Forgive as the Lord forgave you. And over all these virtues put on love, which binds them all together in perfect unity.

Placing ourselves in a position of vulnerability is a reflection of our trust in God to carry us through any challenge we may face, while seeking to share his love. Do you remember the numerous times in the Bible when God raises those who have perceived weakness to positions of real strength? The poor are rich, the lost are found, the blind can see, the lepers are clean, the sick are cured, the lame can walk, the meek will inherit the earth, the humble are the greatest in heaven, the dead have life, and on, and on, and on.

It is all summed up in Christ's Crucifixion. He became the ultimate expression of willingly embracing weakness and submitting to God's plan, making clear the path to eternal life through the power of God's grace.

> 2 Corinthians 13:4.
> Although he was crucified in weakness, he now lives by the power of God ... —NLT

As you can see, the role of a true servant leader is not what many of us are used to seeing or being at work. Weakness as a business virtue? What about authority, wealth, power, and manipulation? "Nice guys finish last" certainly was invoked more than once where I've worked, although it is clear that the "finish" to which the saying refers is the wrong race. Life is indeed an endless marathon.

In the 2009 *New York Times* best-seller *Strengths-Based Leadership* by Tom Rath and Barry Conchie, the authors surveyed over 10,000 people through the Gallup testing organization and concluded that people associate four strengths with outstanding leaders: trust, compassion, stability, and hope. Sound like a leader you know?

These findings reinforce that people are drawn to traits that encourage open communication, mutual support, consistent behavior, and shared goals. Most people are looking to follow leaders whose internal values and beliefs reflect that we are all in this together. You can be that person if you hold on to what you know to be real. Look to your faith as your guide, not external forces, for the values you should emulate, and over time you'll find that others are innately drawn to the truth you represent.

Rest assured that even if you feel you are locked into the most negative, Machiavellian of work environments, you still can be an effective agent of change if you take on the attitude of a servant leader. Jesus was the quintessential agent of change through servant leadership, building the largest religion in the world by incessantly serving others in the face of disbelief and abuse. What he accomplished during his brief ministry, without the aid of modern communication and transportation tools, speaks volumes of the power that underlies true servant leadership.

> 2 Timothy 1:7.
> For God did not give us a spirit of timidity, but a spirit of power, of love and of self-discipline.

Don't be afraid to look outward for opportunities to express the love you have inside you. Remember the source of your love, and rest secure on the strength of the one who is acting through you.

Lead from the Inside Out

Asking "What would Jesus do?" will help you make great decisions throughout your day, but remember to also ask "Why would Jesus do it?" Then you can build the same faith that made his choices the only course he could take.

Go to study sessions:
#8. Serve as He Served, page 103.
#9. Finding Strength in Weakness, page 111.

V

Communities Are the Ultimate Teams

During your professional career you probably have heard it stated that your company places a high value on good teamwork, or that there is no "I" in "TEAM." Teamwork may even be an integral part of your performance appraisal—that's great! Make sure it gets properly reflected in your performance objectives because you are going to be the role model for unselfish teamwork.

It elevates the concept of teamwork when you think of your relationships on the job as part of one community. Healthy communities exert coordinated effort against activities that promote the general welfare of the entire group—mutual benefit is the goal. Basic work teams, on the other hand, start with an external objective and then concentrate on maximizing each other's contribution to achieving that objective.

Both derive their effectiveness from a sense of unity and support, but the underlying motivations and depth of commitment among their respective members differ substantially. Well-functioning communities find motivation in an internally fueled love for one another, while teams seek fulfillment of an externally provided sense of purpose. And while love is a constant, external objectives can be arbitrary and fleeting; therefore, the foundation of the community is deeper, stronger, and more sustainable.

> Romans 12:4–5.
> For as in one body we have many members, and all the members do not have the same function, so we, though many, are one body in Christ, and individually members one of another. —RSV

Individually, God designed us all to complement each other as unique parts of the same community. That is why we find a sense of security and peace as a natural consequence of relationships fueled by mutual concern. This is also something we often seek in our personal relationships at home but usually find more challenging to embrace at work, where we feel more vulnerable due to the dynamics associated with being an individual who has joined a pre-existing corporate body. Still, the same truth applies: professional relationships that focus on fostering collective well-being rather than completing transient activities lead to more lasting expressions of our faith and, as a result, more personal fulfillment.

Embracing our diverse talents, styles, and viewpoints in a climate of mutual support is what helps us attain our collective potential. This means not only allowing others to bring unique skills and perspectives to light but also challenging ourselves to bring our specific contributions to the party. Adopting the vulnerability of the servant leader does not exclude us from leveraging our personal expertise, talents, or knowledge to make noticeable contributions through our job. In fact, our skills have been given to us so we can be effective in all we do, as part of the larger entity.

When we embrace our work as a meaningful part of our lives, it is easy to see how our skills augment those of the people around us. Individually we have potential, but together we have ability.

Ben Davis, a pastor at River Glen Church outside of Milwaukee, likes to communicate the strength of community by saying, "Snowflakes are one of nature's most fragile things, but if enough of them stick together, they can stop traffic." If you are familiar with the periodic harshness of a Great Lakes' winter, you can probably relate to my appreciation of that particular metaphor for strength in numbers!

By building an environment where unique talents are recognized and concern for one another is the normal way of working, you form a flexible network that will naturally protect the group's integrity and maintain its sustainability in the face of adversity. This is a core competency of high-performing teams. It allows members of the team to innately reallocate their combined resources and skills to compensate for unexpected shortfalls and challenges. As a member of such a unique team, this implies you not only need to remain vigilant for opportunities to provide assistance but also for times when you may need to request assistance yourself.

Ecclesiastes 4:9–10.
Two are better than one, because they have a nice return for
their work: If one falls down, his friend can help him up. But
pity the man who falls and has no one to help him up!

The importance of being able to rely on others when things take a turn
toward the unexpected is certainly not lost on me. I have many examples
where impending disasters were turned into occasions for mutual success
and shared growth as a direct result of other individuals jumping in to
save my hide.

In one instance, I had just assumed a newly created position of Vice
President of Innovation, which meant I was accountable for creating an
organization, process, and staff that would deliver step-function advances
in growth for the company. It was a dream job, one I had long aspired to
attain, and I was looking forward to making my mark by overcoming the
challenges of the role, even though it meant commuting from Chicago,
Illinois, to Westport, Connecticut, a good portion of each month for the
foreseeable future.

I was only two months into my new job when reality chose to reassert
itself in the form of Cindi, my wife, being diagnosed with a very aggressive
form of breast cancer. One day I was riding high on my pride; the next day
I was facing the unavoidable realization that our two-year-old son might
soon be wholly dependent upon me to be both mother and father.

In an instant, the job ceased to be my dream. I found a need to share
my situation with my new coworkers so I could rededicate my time, first
and foremost, to my family's welfare and support. This sounds like a no-
brainer in terms of a choice, but at the time it posed a conflict for me,
in that I had not yet fully dedicated myself to the tenets of my professed
Christian faith. My career still held large sway over the values and beliefs
I chose to activate in my life. This made me uneasy about becoming
dependent upon the good will of a new team that was presently engulfed
in the currents of organizational change. My commitment to my family
was assured, but I still had some apprehension about how my career and
financial situation might unravel; full submission to God's plan was not
on my radar.

What I found was that through my vulnerability, others could gain
strength that made our combined ability to succeed even more likely.

Without hesitation my boss made it clear that I could structure my
availability around the demands of Cindi's planned surgeries, chemo, and

other protocols and that I could also drastically slash my time away from Chicago. Because of that support, he reinforced my loyalty and gave rise to one of strongest personal allegiances I hold to date.

Likewise, my newly formed team stepped up and filled the voids that were created by my physical absence over the several months it took to gain stability at home. During those months we all formed stronger bonds with each other as we came to share a common purpose that was rooted in something much more robust than just completing our defined tasks.

This not only improved my ability to effectively delegate, but it also created the foundational trust, respect, and caring that gave rise to a very high-performing, cross-functional group that experienced great success during its tenure and developed closely knit relationships that prosper to this day. Because of our ability as a well-integrated community to compensate for the weakness of one member of our fellowship, we became a unified force that repeatedly achieved excellence and became recognized as a strong group of individual leaders.

In hindsight, I can now appreciate that the key to unlocking the collective strength of the extended team was made possible because we all made the effort to connect in a manner that affirmed our commitment to each other. Clearly, it was love that allowed us to quickly bridge all of our differences, whether religious, racial, lifestyle, or political in nature. This led to our developing the requisite trust that allowed us to fully exploit each other's strengths.

It was also evident that our cohesiveness arose out of my weakness, not my authority. Cindi's bout with cancer had proved to be a positive force, because it provided a vacuum that pulled the good qualities of others to the surface, where they could shine. This taught me the lesson that being open to accepting assistance is equally as important as recognizing opportunities for providing help—you need both to build the linkages that strengthen a community.

Value Individual Strengths

To form a balanced sense of community, we have to recognize and value each other's God-given talents.

> 1 Peter 4:10.
> As each has received a gift, employ it for one another, as good stewards of God's varied grace. —RSV

This is not a new concept. Different functional roles across a company emphasize different skills and capabilities in order to maximize the combined effectiveness of the entire team. We also have long recognized the positive contribution of maintaining cultural and personal diversity in the workplace. We all have something unique that is of value.

The trick is for us as employees to be honest with ourselves about our personal gifts, as well as to truly appreciate the complementary nature of the gifts with which others have been blessed. Avoid developing tunnel vision that only sees what you desire to be, at the expense of understanding what you are really meant to be or in disregard of what others can do better. If everyone who wants to be a CEO was, in fact, in that role, we wouldn't get any work done!

If you manage other people, the onus is squarely on your shoulders to correctly define the needs of each position and assess the strengths of each individual in your charge, so they can be best matched to have maximum impact. Your skill at correctly assessing needs and harnessing your team's innate power is fundamental to being a good steward of the resources you have been entrusted to invest wisely.

Many options exist for assisting with assessing your personal or team strengths. For your convenience, you can find a couple of proven yet inexpensive tools listed in Appendix A, the Additional Resources section of this book. Such assessments can be very constructive, even if you are just curious about your own predispositions, so you can manage your own career so it best emphasizes your strengths.

The 1959 classic movie *Ben Hur* won eleven Academy Awards, including Best Picture. Among all its grandeur, I've always remembered one scene that reinforces the wisdom of focusing on strengths when choosing roles for myself or positioning other people to stand out as exceptional talents in the company.

In the scene, Judah Ben-Hur, played by Charlton Heston, comes upon a sheik training four stunning white Arabian horses on an oval track near an oasis, in preparation for the upcoming chariot races in Rome. As the four horses get up to speed, Judah, an accomplished charioteer himself, comments that they will never hold the turn. Sure enough, the horses fail to complete the turn, careening off the track in a great cloud of dust.

Judah goes on to explain to the sheik that the horses were not harnessed in a manner that capitalized on their individual strengths. Counter to the order in which they had been arranged, Judah recommends that Aldebaran, the swiftest of the horses, should run on the outside, so he can take advantage of his speed to round the corner, and Antares, the most steady of the horses, should take the inside position to better anchor the team as they wheel around the oval.

The recommendation delivers immediate success, and the duly impressed sheik invites Judah to be his charioteer. Long story short: Judah agrees to train the four horses to operate as a single unit and goes on to win the big race in Rome in dramatic fashion.

Judah Ben-Hur knew how to match roles with skills to maximize the overall effectiveness of his group. He wasn't one to waste his time trying to turn a thoroughbred into a plow horse, or a plow horse into a thoroughbred. Instead, he emphasized individual strengths that complemented each other when the whole team was assembled.

From an individual standpoint, it is equally important that you put effort into getting a sense of your primary strengths and motivations. Then you can proactively position yourself to excel as you pursue your purpose, both personally and professionally. Knock yourself out doing what you do best, and don't get sucked into the quagmire of believing that you have to have more of anything—authority, title, money—to succeed. For many of us, the optimal application of our skills and talents may well be what we are currently doing.

In their 1968 book *The Peter Principle,* authors Dr. Laurence J. Peter and Raymond Hull coined a principle that states: "In a hierarchy, every employee tends to rise to his level of incompetence." In other words, you keep getting promoted or moved until you land in a role in which you can't perform. There you stay, to languish or to find your service of no more use to the company, because you are a square peg trying to fit in a round hole.

According to the principle, the incompetence we eventually show as we move up or across the ladder is not necessarily due to the new position being more difficult or to a lack of our intelligence. It is more likely the new role requires a different set of skills than those that made us successful in previous positions. For example, not every Michelin-star chef is talented at running a restaurant, and not every Salesperson of the Year will excel at running a national sales organization.

Our best bet for finding satisfaction at work is to maintain our hope for salvation as our primary reward, remain objective in our assessment of our real gifts, and put forth our best efforts in the spirit of true servant leaders as we move through each day. We can trust that promotions and rewards that reflect our growth during our journey will come as God wills.

It's okay to make yourself open and available for advancement, but avoid measuring your job's value by something you don't already have, and you'll likely find that ever elusive "job satisfaction"!

Celebrate Each Other's Joys

Think of every day as the day of the big game for you and your compatriots at work. Strive to build a well-balanced, cohesive group that respects each other's contributions and shares each other's pains. Likewise, remember to celebrate the wins along the way in order to build and maintain momentum. Once a fire is lit, you have to keep it fed to keep the light burning bright.

> 1 Corinthians 12:24–26.
> But God has so composed the body, giving the greater honor to the inferior part, that there may be no discord in the body, but that the members may have the same care for one another. If one member suffers, all suffer together; if one member is honored, all rejoice together. —RSV

Openly celebrate each other's successes. Be glad for your neighbor's good fortune, and look for ways to bring deserved recognition to those around you. Learning to find joy in each other's achievements and well-being is what builds positive relationships and makes for a unified community. You also greatly multiply your own opportunity to find joy when you allow yourself to share someone else's good fortune. As a result, your professional career will be more fulfilling than remaining a solitary member of a team of which you check in and out at will. Why not be fulfilled in all facets of your life, including the large percentage of your waking hours that you'll spend at work?

> Romans 12:10.
> Love each other with genuine affection, and take delight in honoring each other. —NLT

Have you ever heard people complain that they hate going to work because their contributions are sincerely and openly appreciated? How about because they feel that they are *too* respected? Me, neither. Good things happen when people feel good.

As with giving your love in general, celebrating and serving those around you is not about keeping score on how often you are the servant versus being the recipient. A business would have to be staffed with perfect people with identical perspectives to achieve equivalent reciprocity. That will never be the case, nor is it a prerequisite to share God's love.

It is more important that you have faith that you will make it possible for others to move forward through an honest expression of the spirit that leads you. When you measure your lifetime's achievement by the collective salvation of all, the absence of a few personally directed praises during your professional career bears no value in comparison.

Internal Inspiration Is Stronger than External Expectation

Are your activities at work defined by external objectives or internal motivations? Do you look at the activities you need to complete as things to benefit others or just tasks to get done? Caring about those around you will provide a sense that your job's outputs are helping you achieve your greater purpose in life.

Begin by openly celebrating the success of someone you work with this week.

Go to study session:
#10. One Community, page 115.

VI

Communication Counts

Relying on our faith for inspiration enhances our relationships by actively sharing our love in an unconditional manner. As a result, we seek to facilitate the development of an environment that maintains a sense of shared purpose, unselfish support, and mutual trust, where we can all prosper and enjoy work as part of our overall lives.

To be successful in this endeavor, our ability to effectively convey our love as a servant leader will be dependent upon our words as much as our actions; therefore, good communication practices are fundamental to understanding and developing synergies with our fellow employees.

Although it would be wonderful if our words were always interpreted as having positive meaning, the fact is that sometimes we say things that can have a negative effect on our relationships.

> James 3:2.
> Indeed we all make mistakes. For if we could control our tongues, we would be perfect and could also control ourselves in every other way. —NLT

Our flaws are bound to come out in our words; thus, a realistic goal is to maximize positive and stop negative communication practices as much as possible. Given that objective, this chapter will focus on solid advice found in the New Testament with respect to managing our tongues.

Keep it Constructive

Ask a person if he believes feedback can be constructive, and he'll invariably say yes. Ask the same person if all feedback he gets is constructive, and the reality is he'll probably say no.

Not only is it difficult for the provider of the feedback to always speak the truth in love to the intended recipient, but it is also common for the recipient to mistrust the real intent of the message. This speaks again to the importance of creating a sense of community, so both parties trust in each other's motivations when they communicate with each another.

This also leads to defining constructive feedback as "Feedback that is based in love with the intention of facilitating improvement or development"—the assumption being that it is both given *and* received with a positive spirit.

Effectively giving and receiving constructive feedback is widely seen as the holy grail of performance reviews, but the benefits of constructive feedback are too large to restrict its application to the small amount of time we dedicate in most companies to formal reviews. Better that it should be a standard way of communicating with one another as part of our normal routines.

> Ephesians 4:29.
> Do not let any unwholesome talk come out of your mouths, but only what is helpful for building others up according to their needs, that it may benefit those who listen.

The above verse from Ephesians reinforces the need for two-way participation to make feedback constructive. Whether the communication is going up, down, across, or outside the organization, both parties need to play their part to make it a positive experience. The same also holds true for all forms of providing counsel, accountability, and encouragement.

As inspired leaders, the call for us is to be role models who keep a positive tone to the exchange. When providing feedback, base it in love. When receiving feedback, assume positive intent.

Avoid Fires

In practice, the benefit realized from constructive feedback is highly dependent upon how close the perceptions, values, and beliefs of the giver mirror those of the receiver. No two people are identical, even if they share the same faith; therefore, you can count on disagreements and strife to occasionally surface as a direct result of something you do or say during your career. The key is to be cognizant of when your good intentions are likely to have negative consequences so you can adjust to the realities of the situation.

> 2 Timothy 2:23–25.
> Don't have anything to do with foolish and stupid arguments, because you know they produce quarrels. And the Lord's servant must not quarrel; instead, he must be kind to everyone, able to teach, not resentful. [25]Those who oppose him he must gently instruct, in the hope that God will grant them repentance leading them to a knowledge of the truth.

A good habit for maintaining stable relations is to put our emphasis on listening, not just hearing, so we can better empathize with the speaker and avoid responsively lashing out in anger. Even then, we may not like what is being said or the style in which it is presented. In these situations, taking time to respond is a recommended course of action.

> James 1:19.
> Everyone should be quick to listen, slow to speak and slow to become angry.

This is consistent with both the ten-second rule and twenty-four-hour rule—waiting ten seconds before responding verbally during tense face-to-face situations and waiting twenty-four hours before responding to frustrating e-mails or voicemails. No wonder this works!

The good news is that when we foster a sense of community, an open line of communication naturally evolves that makes it possible to both contribute and accept constructive points of view. It also provides the feelings of trust and shared commitment that makes it possible for the members of a group to move past the occasional slight.

> Matthew 18:15–16.
> If your brother sins against you, go and show him his fault, just between the two of you. If he listens to you, you have won your brother over. But if he will not listen, take one or two others along, so that "every matter may be established by the testimony of two or three witnesses."

It is obviously preferable for two people to work out their differences whenever possible, but the jury-of-peers approach is also a viable option. In any case, the key point is that both of the directly involved parties are engaged in the deliberation and the solution. If you are one of the parties involved, proactively seek resolution of the issue through the applicable process for your situation.

In the meantime, avoid unfairly slandering the other party when he is not present to state his case. Such comments likely will only inflame the situation and give the impression that you are selfishly seeking to misconstrue the real facts. Either way, you will destroy what you are aspiring to create as a servant leader. For this reason, a well-functioning community or effective manager will discourage unilateral complaints and make it clear that he or she will remain unbiased until he or she collects facts from all involved.

Gossip, guile, and malice are close relatives of slander that also relish lurking in the shadows of even the closest of teams. Most of us find perverse appeal to either sharing or hearing "good dirt" on somebody. Whatever the reason, the recommended course of action is to quell such discussions.

> 1 Peter 2:1.
> Therefore, rid yourselves of all malice and all deceit, hypocrisy, envy, and slander of every kind.

The formula appears simple: minimize communication that leads to negative results, and maximize communication that has a positive outcome, yet the challenge of doing so is not easy. It is one that requires heightened awareness and real diligence to complete. It also remains dependent upon creating a shared value system among all the parties involved to ensure a shared interpretation of intent.

Overall, it begins with why you say what you say or hear what you hear. As long as you remain true to deriving your motivation and response from the continual expression of God's love, you will habitually keep vigilant against stimulating discord.

Good Communication Implies Shared Understanding

Think about an extended dialogue (e-mail, phone, or in person) you recently had at work. How would you describe:
1. your underlying motivations for the conversation?
2. the other party's perception of your motivations?
3. the common beliefs and values you share with the other party?

Now think about how you can improve on all three points prior to engaging in your next conversation with either the same party or someone new. Make your improvements part of your ongoing way of building effective two-way communication.

Go to study session:
#11. Good Communication Makes for Good Communities, page 120.

VII

Endurance 'til the End

For the millions of people who have seen their savings depleted or positions eliminated, the fallacy of looking to the status and income generated by one's career for a sense of purpose is self-evident. Like everything terrestrial, the feelings of professional fulfillment and financial security that we get from work have an unpredictable ebb and flow as well.

Faith does not suffer from the same turmoil. In fact, challenging events serve to strengthen our faith by reinforcing that we have a constant promise we can rely on for support. When we find our inspiration through God's Word, not through our job descriptions, the outcomes we experience because of our jobs are much more fulfilling and enduring.

> Romans 5:3–5.
> More than that, we rejoice in our sufferings, knowing that suffering produces endurance and endurance produces character, and character produces hope, and hope does not disappoint us, because God's love has been poured into our hearts through the Holy Spirit which has been given to us.

Romans 5:3–5 rings especially true with my family. We recognize that our personal challenges renewed our search for the truth in God's Word and strengthened our resolve to hold on to it going forward. Sometimes we have to get lost in the dark before we remember the value of a good flashlight! Gratefully, we were able to find the light we had left behind in time for it to guide us through the continual onslaught of challenging circumstances that are commonly faced during one's lifetime.

The death of my father, followed by Cindi's battle with triple-negative breast cancer (now seven years in remission), my oldest sister's death, and the death of my mother were big eye-openers that we are not in control. They also gave Cindi and me pause during our hectic pursuit of professional success, and we considered the real strength of our professed faith. Did we really understand what it meant to die? Were we really on the right path to accomplish what we are meant to accomplish in this life? Did we really believe everything in the Bible, or had we interpreted it to accommodate our desired lifestyle? Mortality provides excellent ballast for stabilizing one's perspective of life.

Thanks largely to these events, we finally began to shift our focus from pursuing more stuff to better appreciating God's purpose for us as Christians—and just in time, because almost immediately after my sister's death we were faced with new challenges that are also familiar to many other families; the challenges of participating in the effects of a collapsing economy. We went almost two years without any real income, saw our savings dramatically slashed, and shed some of our stuff, including our house, in order to protect against a protracted downturn in the economy.

Thanks to the fact that God had previously opened our hearts to understanding and accepting his unfailing love for us, we actually found our faith and our happiness growing stronger during these latest challenges— so much so that it was during those times I found the inspiration for this book.

I can now more fully relate to the oft-stated quote: "That which doesn't break you makes you stronger." It is also clear that this saying echoes Romans 5:3–5, referenced above. Endurance is a key ingredient to growth, because it is a surety that during our lives we all will encounter circumstances that can be used to strengthen our underlying character and reinforce our reliance on the hope we secure through real belief in Jesus as our Lord and Savior. That which happens in this lifetime is but a prod that drives us toward our final goal.

Endurance is not a rare concept in today's society. We often positively associate it with people who have the ability to sustain hardships and adversity in the face of great challenges. It is also one of the reasons athletes hold celebrity status, because they are recognized as having the fortitude and commitment to use obstacles to shape their overall prowess at a given sport.

One athlete I know, John MacLean, became a paraplegic at age twenty-two as the result of a traffic accident. June 27, 1998, he was riding his bike on the shoulder of a motorway in his native Australia when he was struck by the inattentive driver of a white eight-ton truck doing 66 miles an hour. The resulting injuries John suffered where catastrophic—multiple breaks in his back, pelvis, ribs, sternum, and arm; and head trauma, hemorrhages, and punctures in both lungs that would give rise to a near-fatal bout with pneumonia. The accident scene was horrific, so much so that the priest, who was one of the first people on the scene, gave John the last rites. The staff at the hospital was equally resigned to his imminent death. But they were all mistaken. John would recover after a long rehabilitation, during which time he adjusted to his new life without the use of his legs.

Since his accident, John has gone on to become the first wheelchair athlete to complete the twenty-six-mile swim across the English Channel. He is also the first to complete Hawaii's Iron Man Triathlon. He even earned recognition in the Hawaiian Iron Man Hall of Fame after mastering the grueling 2.4-mile swim, 112-mile bike ride, and 26.2-mile marathon within the established qualifying time set for "able-bodied" participants. More recently, John succeeded in winning a silver medal in the TA2X Adaptive Rowing competition with his partner, Kathryn Ross, at the 2008 Beijing Paralympic Games. The list goes on. But all stats aside, John has repeatedly demonstrated that one can find the strength and will within himself to overcome adversity in order to pursue a goal.

Exceptional athletes not only persevere when they encounter physical and mental fatigue, but they also invite these challenges through their actions, knowing that these challenges have to be endured in order to achieve their goals.

Achieving our goal as Christians does not require the same physical endurance, but the internal commitment required in terms of mental awareness and submission to God's will can be much greater, requiring a lifetime of performance in the face of daily challenges.

Hebrews 10:36.
Patient endurance is what you need now, so that you will continue to do God's will. Then you will receive all that he has promised.
—NLT

Because our race is long, we also are well advised to borrow a page from the training programs of successful athletes who benefit from having coaches, trainers, and partners to keep them encouraged and accountable during their chosen journey. Even the greatest of athletes needs a little help to become his or her very best. The need is even greater for the person who is seeking to achieve a calling that requires a lifetime of commitment.

Forming bonds with other people who share our values will help us find encouragement when we need it and reinforce that we are part of a bigger plan. The more people helping, the easier it is to carry the load. This is where small groups and fellowship with like-minded Christians can really play a vital role in our life.

By actively forming connections with others who demonstrate they share our values, both at home and at work, we will also find that together, we will maintain better accountability for our respective actions. As a result, we will be more successful at creating the positive work environment we seek to foster.

> Hebrews 10:23–24.
> Let us hold unswervingly to the hope we profess, for he who promised is faithful. And let us consider how we may spur one another on toward love and good deeds.

Don't try to slug it out alone, and don't make the mistake of thinking that listening to a sermon as a member of a Sunday congregation is a substitute for proactively maintaining ongoing connections with like-minded Christians. Maintaining two-way dialogue with people who can readily engage with you in your daily life will greatly strengthen your resolve.

Watching ESPN's *Sport Center* does not make you a great athlete. Likewise, cheering for Christ from the side-lines is not the same as being a Christian.

Even if your support network is not composed of people you work with, you will find that through your network's support and encouragement, you will better keep your overall purpose in front of you and lessen the ability of the world's conflicting pressures to wear you down. We are all in this battle together.

Perhaps no one will ever return any semblance of concern for your personal situation, but does that mean you give up? No. It means you need to keep your light visible in the hope that others will come to see the value in what God is offering through you. Maybe you are just intended to plant mustard seeds that won't blossom until another Christian does the watering.

Hold on to the hope that your reward lies at the end of it all and that each challenge is only meant to strengthen your resolve to remain faithful.

As long as you find joy and peace in the motivation for your choices, you will find fulfillment.

Submission to God's Will Extends to Submission to Authority

For the 99.9 percent of us who are accountable to someone of higher rank in a corporate hierarchy, leading with our faith also means gladly performing our appointed roles as directed by those who have been given the authority to lead us. Line managers, senior executives, government agencies, team owners, outside investors, etc.—lots of constituencies exist that have been empowered to make decisions that directly influence tasks we are then expected to perform, regardless of our personal view of the situation.

> 1 Peter 2:18.
> Servants, be submissive to your masters with all respect, not only to the kind but also to the overbearing. —RSV

Willingly accepting direction from earthly leaders is part of God's plan, but adopting values and beliefs counter to your faith is not. Don't wrongly assume that because you report to someone of higher authority that you lack the necessary influence to improve circumstances from your current position or that things would be better if you were in charge. These lead you down the false path of believing that you do not presently have at your disposal all you need to find fulfillment.

In reality, you are in charge ... of yourself. Apply your God-given talents and abilities to share his love and serve others. That is the task at hand for all inspired leaders. Recognize the power this provides you to enact positive change and the strength it provides you to persevere and overcome obstacles.

Always remember that the source of your inspiration comes from one who showed that any trial can be endured if you remain steadfast in the spirit that leads you and keep your sights on the prize you seek. Don't be diverted from your chosen purpose in life by the negative influences of people and circumstances around you. Resting your hope in the true value of God's grace puts everything in perspective.

> 1 Peter 1:6–7.
> So be truly glad. There is wonderful joy ahead, even though you have to endure many trials for a little while. These trials

will show that your faith is genuine. It is being tested as fire tests and purifies gold—though your faith is far more precious than mere gold. So when your faith remains strong through many trials, it will bring you much praise and glory and honor on the day when Jesus Christ is revealed to the whole world.
—NLT

Stay focused on why you make your choices; then how you act will represent your faith-based motivations and resolve. And in the end, you will attain your goal as you work with real purpose and join God at work.

Illuminate Hope

Hope in our guaranteed future helps us weather all adversities and pulls us forward through this life. Illuminating that hope for others to see is something we can all do as Christians to help others come to value that which we share. But always keeping true to our potential is no easy task. We all need each other to bring out our best.

On whom can you rely to help you strengthen your trust in God's plan? Set up a regular time to check in with that person or group for support and accountability.

Go to study session:
#12. Hope and Endurance, page 124.

Afterword

Born anew.

Continuing the Journey

Going forward, I love to think that the amount of mutual support we all find at work will somehow grow exponentially as a result of letting our faith be the source of our inspiration. But more important, I pray that we keep our work in its proper place as subordinate to our primary purpose in life: to help others come to see God's glory and accept his grace through their actively expressing their belief in Jesus Christ as our Lord and Savior.

Real belief will motivate each of us to make the right choices, beginning with our personal commitment to shed our old self and adopt the new life that is life indeed.

> Romans 6:3–4
> Or have you forgotten that when we were joined with Christ Jesus in baptism, we joined him in his death? For we died and were buried with Christ by baptism. And just as Christ was raised from the dead by the glorious power of the Father, now we also may live new lives. —NLT

May we all take the step of affirming our belief through baptism and acceptance of his gift of the Holy Spirit, so God can work through us as we willingly fulfill his purpose for us. In the meantime, I am thankful he allowed me this chance to share his love as best I could.

Be Inspired

For each of us, our values and beliefs give rise to our actions. When our faith inspires our actions, our actions reflect the positive aspects of Christian values. When worldly considerations motivate us, we display the flaws inherent in the source. Because none of us is perfect, expect to show both. But take the challenging step of inventorying how deeply you are presently influenced by God's Word versus the world's view.

Have you committed yourself through baptism to shedding the ways of the world? If not, continue to seek understanding and purpose from God. You can trust he'll put it in your heart when you're ready. If you have been baptized, are you sharing the love you represent? Remember that Christ is looking for us to be followers, not just fans. We all play a part in God's plan. What will your role be?

Go to study session:
#13. Baptism and the Holy Spirit, page 130.

Borrowing from Johann Sebastian Bach's customary sign-off:

Soli Deo Gloria
(For the Glory of God Alone)

STUDY GUIDE

Inspired Work:
A New Testament Guide to Working with Purpose

Study time.

Introduction

This companion study guide is intended to help bridge the large chasm that exists between the primary points made in the book *Inspired Work: A New Testament Guide to Working with Purpose* and the depth of spiritual strength and practical knowledge found in the Bible. While the book focuses on introducing a few biblical themes, illustrated with relevant examples from the workplace, the study guide moves one step closer to the source by placing greater reliance on scriptural reflection to allow you to let God's Words directly speak to you in the context of your own work experience and Christian development.

Ideally, you will share your journey with others as you walk through the study guide so that you can mutually build up each other during your quest. The premise is that small groups form a safe platform from which each individual can build momentum behind his resolve to rely on his faith to guide him while at work. Specifically, the format of each study session proceeds as follows:

- Study sessions are designed to build on specific chapters.
- Scriptural verses referenced in the book are restated at the beginning of each study session, so you have an easy link back to the main themes.
- Additional verses are provided to reinforce the concepts covered in the book and to introduce new topics that have contextual relevance.
- Questions are provided to facilitate personal reflection and group discussion.

The power of the truth conveyed by the verses referenced herein is evidenced by the consistency with which their themes are communicated throughout the Scriptures. Reading the verses will establish awareness of their relevance to your professional life, but adopting them as part of your guiding faith is where their benefit really lies. Keep in mind this is not a *how*-to book; rather, it's a *why*-to book!

Allowing time for proper reflection on how it all comes together for you will greatly enhance your ability to find new avenues for spiritual growth.

Most importantly, remember that the ultimate source of the motivation and resolve we are seeking comes from God; therefore, prayer, both individually and for each other, is the one ingredient that will best improve your ability to find your leadership inspiration in your Christian faith.

Recommended Pairing of Book Chapters with Study Sessions

Study sessions are intended to reinforce the themes covered in the book in a cumulative fashion. Because of this, it is recommended that the complementary study sessions be completed after each chapter in the following order:

Book Chapter	Theme	Study Session	Title
Preface	Personal inspiration	1	The Universal Truth
Introduction	Work as part of life's purpose; not distinct	2	Faith Applies to All We Do
1	Faith gives rise to hope which focuses us on our goal.	3	Faith and Submission to God's Will
2	Love is the engine that brings faith to life	4	All with Love
2		5	Faith Trumps Law
3	Faith finds its beginning in you and expression through you	6	All Christians are Called to be Leaders
3		7	Faith Is an Active State
4	Christians are servant leaders	8	Servant Leadership
4		9	Strength in Weakness
5	Communities are the ultimate teams	10	One Community
6	Communication counts	11	Good Communities Communicate

Book Chapter	Theme	Study Session	Title
7	Endurance 'til the end	12	Hope and Endurance
Afterword	Concluding thoughts	13	Baptism and the Holy Spirit

By building each tier in order, you will find each subsequent tier is more easily related back to the first principles covered, helping fuel the momentum and confidence that will carry you through to the end.

Our Source of Truth

Find the Truth

Study Session 1

The Universal Truth

Verse quoted in the preface of the book:

John 14:6.
Jesus answered, "I am the way and the truth and the life. No one comes to the Father except through me."

For Christians, the truth is found in God's Word. It is our universal framework for understanding reality. It also provides us with shared views of right and wrong—then, now, and forever—which allow us to share a unified existence.

Consider the alternative. Without a universal truth, you cannot have a universal definition for right and wrong. As a result, each individual would be allowed to create arbitrary definitions of right and wrong based upon his or her own perceptions of reality; you would have no basis for an endurable shared value system. If this were the case, ever-changing public opinion and outright anarchy would become customary paths to establishing the truth and defining what is acceptable and what isn't. Because no two people share the same perceptions or beliefs, one would have to impose his own value system on others in order to drive social conformity under the banner of his own choosing. Likewise, definitions of right, wrong, and truth would be fluid, changing dramatically over both time and distance.

Luckily, we don't have to devolve into a never-ending I'm right/you're wrong debate to establish lasting principles of right or wrong. God provides the answer for us all, so we can just get on with living our lives as he intended, once we accept the truth of his word and take it to heart.

It is important to recognize we all differ in our journeys to becoming good Christians, thanks to the unique forces that have been put in our lives to help shape us as we grow over time. Regardless of these differences, personally accepting that God's Word is the ultimate source of truth is necessary if this study guide is to accomplish its purpose. Having that common foundation allows us to be of like mind and shared spirit as we move forward through personal reflection, mutual support, and sincere prayer.

With all of this in mind, we start with a sample of New Testament Scriptures on the subject of "Truth" to help reinforce how central wholeheartedly trusting God's Word is to the Christian faith.

God's Word Is Truth

John 17:17.
Sanctify them by the truth; your word is truth.

James 1:18.
He chose to give us birth through the word of truth …

John 8:47.
He who belongs to God hears what God says. The reason you do not hear is that you do not belong to God.

Jesus Plays a Pivotal Role in the Truth

John 18:37.
"You are a king, then!" said Pilate. Jesus answered, "You are right in saying I am a king. In fact, for this reason I was born, and for this I came into the world, to testify to the truth. Everyone on the side of truth listens to me."

Romans 10:9.
That if you confess with your mouth, "Jesus is Lord," and believe in your heart that God raised him from the dead, you will be saved.

2 Thessalonians 2:13.
But we ought always to thank God for you, brothers loved by the Lord, because from the beginning God chose you to be saved through the sanctifying work of the Spirit and through belief in the truth.

1 John 5:9–11.

We accept human testimony, but God's testimony is greater because it is the testimony of God, which he has given about his Son. Whoever believes in the Son of God accepts this testimony. Whoever does not believe God has made him out to be a liar, because they have not believed the testimony God has given about his Son. And this is the testimony: God has given us eternal life, and this life is in his Son.

John 8:31–32.

To the Jews who had believed him, Jesus said, "If you hold to my teaching, you are really my disciples. Then you will know the truth, and the truth will set you free."

Expect the Truth to Be Challenged

2 Peter 2:1–3.

But false prophets also arose among the people … and because of them the truth will be reviled … —RSV

Jude 1:18–19.

They said to you, "In the last times there will be scoffers who will follow their own ungodly desires." These are the men who divide you, who follow mere natural instincts and do not have the Spirit.

2 Timothy 4:3–4.

For the time will come when men will not put up with sound doctrine. Instead, to suit their own desires, they will gather around them a great number of teachers to say what their itching ears want to hear. They will turn their ears away from the truth and turn aside to myths.

2 Timothy 3:1–5.

But mark this: There will be terrible times in the last days. People will be lovers of themselves, lovers of money, boastful, proud, abusive, disobedient to their parents, ungrateful, unholy, without love, unforgiving, slanderous, without self-control, brutal, not lovers of the good, treacherous, rash, conceited, lovers of pleasure rather than lovers of God—having a form of godliness but denying its power. Have nothing to do with them.

2 Thessalonians 2:9–10.
The coming of the lawless one will be in accordance with the work of Satan displayed in all kinds of counterfeit miracles, signs and wonders, and in every sort of evil that deceives those who are perishing. They perish because they refused to love the truth and so be saved.

Trust Your Faith to Overcome the World's Influences

Colossians 2:8.
See to it that no one takes you captive through hollow and deceptive philosophy, which depends on human tradition and the basic principles of this world rather than on Christ.

1 John 4:2–3.
This is how you can recognize the Spirit of God: Every spirit that acknowledges that Jesus Christ has come in the flesh is from God, but every spirit that does not acknowledge Jesus is not from God. This is the spirit of the antichrist, which you have heard is coming and even now is already in the world.

2 Peter 3:17–18.
Therefore, dear friends, since you already know this, be on your guard so that you may not be carried away by the error of lawless men and fall from your secure position. But grow in the grace and knowledge of our Lord and Savior Jesus Christ.

Ephesians 4:14–15.
Then we will no longer be infants, tossed back and forth by the waves, and blown here and there by every wind of teaching and by the cunning and craftiness of men in their deceitful scheming. Instead, speaking the truth in love, we will in all things grow up into him who is the Head, that is, Christ.

1 Corinthians 1:18.
For the message of the cross is foolishness to those who are

perishing, but to us who are being saved it is the power of God.

See also: Luke 8:4–15, the Parable of the Seeds of Faith.

Questions for Discussion:

1. How do you define the meaning of the word "truth"?

2. Do you believe that the Bible provides the foundation for *real* truth?

3. How much of your time is spent exposed to God's Word vs. other views?

4. What impact has this had in shaping the guiding principles of your faith?

5. What are examples of competing truths in today's world?

6. Where do you personally struggle to believe in the Bible's teachings?

7. How can you become more strongly grounded in what is true?

8. What impact do you expect this to have on how you approach your job?

Note: Recommended for additional study: Focus on the Family's *The Truth Project* by Dr. Del Tackett, a twelve-part series available in DVD format and designed for use with small groups. It's excellent for wrapping your mind around the fundamental question of "What is truth?" For more information go to *www.TheTruthProject.com*.

Part I
The Leap of Faith

Take the leap.

Study Session 2

Faith Applies to All We Do

Verses quoted in the introduction to the book:

Romans 8:28.
And we know that in all things God works for the good of those who love him, who have been called according to his purpose.

Colossians 3:23–4.
Whatever you do, work at it with all your heart, as working for the Lord, not for men, since you know that you will receive an inheritance from the Lord as a reward. It is the Lord Christ you are serving.

When our view of the world begins and ends with our faith for inspiration and fulfillment, the verses above make a lot of sense. Real faith is both omnipresent and palpable. It is not something we keep stored until we need it, nor is it something that only has relevance to part of our lives. It is sitting inside us, waiting for expression through all we say and do.

When you walk through your day with faith, you literally walk with Christ, and he gladly makes himself known if you let him. Remember that your faith is there to help you, twenty-four hours a day—let it! You will find it gives real purpose to everything in your life, even work!

Consider the following Scriptures for additional reflection:

Faith Is Relevant to All We Do

2 Timothy 3:16–17.
All Scripture is God-breathed and is useful for teaching, rebuking, correcting and training in righteousness, so that

the man of God may be thoroughly equipped for every good work.

1 Timothy 1:19.
Cling to your faith in Christ, and keep your conscience clear. For some people have deliberately violated their consciences; as a result, their faith has been shipwrecked.

2 Timothy 2:15.
Do your best to present yourself to God as one approved, a workman who does not need to be ashamed and who correctly handles the word of truth.

John 6:28–29.
Then they asked him, "What must we do to do the works God requires?" Jesus answered, "The work of God is this: to believe in the one he has sent."

Real Faith Can Only Inspire Good Intentions

John 10:10.
The thief comes only to steal and kill and destroy; I have come that they may have life, and have it to the full.

John 10:37–38.
Do not believe me unless I do what my Father does. But if I do it, even though you do not believe me, believe the miracles, that you may know and understand that the Father is in me, and I in the Father.

Ephesians 2:10.
For we are God's workmanship, created in Christ Jesus to do good works, which God prepared in advance for us to do.

Philippians 2:13.
For it is God who works in you to will and to act in order to fulfill his good purpose.

Questions for Discussion:

1. How important is your job to defining who you are?

2. Does your job support or define your overall purpose in life? How?

3. Can acting in accordance with your faith be negative?

4. In what ways do you currently rely on your faith to provide guidance for your actions at work?

5. What opportunities will you have next week to rely on your faith to guide your interactions with others?

Study Session 3

Faith and Submission to God's Will

Verses quoted in chapter 1 of the book:

Hebrews 11:1.
Now faith is being sure of what we hope for and certain of what we do not see.

1 Peter 1:8–9.
Though you have not seen him, you love him; and even though you do not see him now, you believe in him and are filled with an inexpressible and glorious joy, for you are receiving the goal of your faith, the salvation of your souls.

Luke 6:47–48.
I will show you what he is like who comes to me and hears my words and puts them into practice. He is like a man building a house, who dug down deep and laid the foundation on rock. ...

Romans 12:2.
Don't copy the behavior and customs of this world, but let God transform you into a new person by changing the way you think. Then you will learn to know God's will for you, which is good and pleasing and perfect. —NLT

Matthew 26:39.
Going a little farther, he fell with his face to the ground and prayed, "My Father, if it is possible, may this cup be taken from me. Yet not as I will, but as you will."

Everything begins and ends with Christ. Therefore, all our actions are intended to begin and end with him as our source of inspiration. By drawing on the strength that comes with acceptance of what he has given us, we are then armed with the knowledge and wisdom to avoid being led by falsehoods.

Strengthening our faith provides the hope that will pull us through everything we experience in our lifetime. It also provides the lifeline that we can hold on to as we go about our daily lives. Although I focus attention in this study guide on the way in which applying a faith-based leadership perspective can strengthen our growth and value at work, the underlying goal is to reinforce our commitment to making our faith central to all we do. In the end, finding our motivation in our faith will help make us more complete Christians and increase our benefit to others.

The Scriptures below provide a brief outline of how the New Testament defines faith and why it is important in our lives. We also will see additional verses that reinforce how real faith comes from willingly submitting to God's will.

The concept of submission should not be misinterpreted as a negative action. Remember that just as parents lovingly expect their children to submit to the parents' better judgment, we should also find it natural to accept that our heavenly Father's judgment is far superior to our own. Regardless of our age or experience, God knows best.

As always, consider going to the source to gain a fuller appreciation of the spirit behind the words as you read the following verses.

Faith Provides Our Sense of Purpose

Hebrews 11:6.
And without faith it is impossible to please God, because anyone who comes to him must believe that he exists and that he rewards those who earnestly seek him.

2 Corinthians 5:7.
We live by faith, not by sight.

2 Corinthians 4:18.
So we fix our eyes not on what is seen, but on what is unseen. For what is seen is temporary, but what is unseen is eternal.

John 20:29.
Then Jesus told him, "Because you have seen me, you have

believed; blessed are those who have not seen and yet have believed."

Luke 8:48.
Then he said to her, "Daughter, your faith has healed you. Go in peace."

Hope of Salvation Keeps Us on Course

Romans 15:13.
May the God of hope fill you with all joy and peace as you trust in him, so that you may overflow with hope by the power of the Holy Spirit.

John 14:19–20.
Before long, the world will not see me anymore, but you will see me. Because I live, you also will live. On that day you will realize that I am in my Father, and you are in me, and I am in you.

1 Peter 1:13.
Therefore, prepare your minds for action; be self-controlled; set your hope fully on the grace to be given you when Jesus Christ is revealed.

1 Peter 1:21.
Through him you believe in God, who raised him from the dead and glorified him, and so your faith and hope are in God.

Romans 8:24–25.
For in this hope we were saved. But hope that is seen is no hope at all. Who hopes for what he already has? But if we hope for what we do not yet have, we wait for it patiently.

Attaining Both Requires Humility and Acceptance of God's Will

John 6:38.
For I have come down from heaven not to do my will but to do the will of him who sent me.

2 Corinthians 1:9.
Indeed, in our hearts we felt the sentence of death. But this happened that we might not rely on ourselves but on God, who raises the dead.

John: 12:24.
Truly, truly, I say to you, unless a grain of wheat falls into the earth and dies, it remains alone; but if it dies, it bears much fruit.

Matthew 16:25.
For whoever wants to save his life will lose it, but whoever loses his life for me will find it.

James 4:7–8.
Submit yourselves, then, to God. Resist the devil, and he will flee from you. Come near to God and he will come near to you. …

1 Peter 1:14.
As obedient children, do not conform to the evil desires you had when you lived in ignorance. But just as he who called you is holy, so be holy in all you do.

Mark 10:15.
I tell you the truth, anyone who will not receive the kingdom of God like a little child will never enter it.

You Can Trust God to Care for Your Best Interests

1 Peter 5:7.
Cast all your anxiety on him because he cares for you.

Matthew 11:28.
Come to me, all you who are weary and burdened, and I will give you rest.

John 14:27.
Peace I leave with you; my peace I give you. I do not give to you as the world gives. Do not let your hearts be troubled and do not be afraid.

Philippians 4:6–7.
Do not be anxious about anything, but in everything, by prayer and petition, with thanksgiving, present your requests to God. And the peace of God, which transcends all understanding, will guard your hearts and your minds in Christ Jesus.

Matthew 6:25–26, 33. "Therefore I tell you, do not worry about your life, what you will eat or drink; or about your body, what you will wear. Is not life more important than food, and the body more important than clothes? Look at the birds of the air; they do not sow or reap or store away in barns, and yet your heavenly Father feeds them. Are you not much more valuable than they?" ... [33]But seek first his kingdom and his righteousness, and all these things will be given to you as well.

Matthew 6:34.
Therefore do not worry about tomorrow, for tomorrow will worry about itself. Each day has enough trouble of its own.

Questions for Discussion:

1. On a scale of 1 to 10, with 10 being perfect, how strong is your faith?

2. How often do you encounter views that conflict with your faith?

3. How do you reconcile differences between scriptural teachings and conflicting viewpoints?

4. Do you have any examples of incorporating worldly influences into your faith?

5. Do you find it easier to submit to superiors at work or to submit to God's will?

6. How do they differ?

7. Which leads to greater unity and reward?

8. What barriers in your life do you have to address to make it easier for you to trust God?

9. How much time can you commit each week to actively spending time with God?

Study Session 4

All with Love

Verses quoted in the first half of chapter 2:

Matthew 22:37–40.
Jesus replied: "Love the Lord your God with all your heart and with all your soul and with all your mind." This is the first and greatest commandment. And the second is like it: "Love your neighbor as yourself." All the Law and the Prophets hang on these two commandments.

1 Corinthians 13:4–7.
Love is patient, love is kind. It does not envy, it does not boast, it is not proud. It is not rude, it is not self-seeking, it is not easily angered, it keeps no record of wrongs. Love does not delight in evil but rejoices with the truth. It always protects, always trusts, always hopes, always perseveres.

1 Corinthians 13:1–3.
If I speak in the tongues of men and of angels, but have not love, I am only a resounding gong or a clanging cymbal. If I have the gift of prophecy and can fathom all mysteries and all knowledge, and if I have a faith that can move mountains, but have not love, I am nothing. If I give all I possess to the poor and surrender my body to the flames, but have not love, I gain nothing.

1 Peter 3:8–9.
Finally, all of you, live in harmony with one another; be sympathetic, love as brothers, be compassionate and humble. Do not repay evil with evil or insult with insult, but with

blessing, because to this you were called so that you may inherit a blessing.

When we are young we are taught that sharing is a good practice. As we grow up, we realize this is true on many levels. So by the time we are parents, it's natural to tell our own children to share what they long to keep to themselves. We know they will benefit more from sharing their precious belongings than from withholding them from others.

The same applies to our faith. We have been given something of value by our Father in heaven, and he wants us to understand it is meant to be shared. The love he has for us exists for the benefit of all. Let's not hoard our belongings like untrained children. Let's follow our own advice and share from the bottomless pool of love he has put inside us.

The Golden Rule Rules

1 Corinthians 16:14.
Do everything in love.

Luke 10:27.
He answered: "Love the Lord your God with all your heart and with all your soul and with all your strength and with all your mind"; and, "Love your neighbor as yourself."

John 15:12.
My command is this: Love each other as I have loved you.

James 2:8.
If you really fulfill the royal law, according to the scripture, 'You shall love your neighbor as yourself,' you do well.
—RSV

Hebrews 13:1–2.
Keep on loving each other as brothers. Do not forget to entertain strangers, for by so doing some people have entertained angels without knowing it.

1 John 4:7–8.
Dear friends, let us love one another, for love comes from God. Everyone who loves has been born of God and knows

God. Whoever does not love does not know God, because God is love.

Love Is the Sincere Expression of Faith

1 John 3:18.
Dear children, let us not love with words or tongue but with actions and in truth.

1 Timothy 1:5.
The goal of this command is love, which comes from a pure heart and a good conscience and a sincere faith.

Luke 7:47.
Therefore, I tell you, her many sins have been forgiven—for she loved much. But he who has been forgiven little loves little.

2 Peter 1:5–7.
For this reason make every effort to supplement your faith with virtue, and virtue with knowledge, and knowledge with self-control, and self-control with steadfastness, and steadfastness with godliness, and godliness with brotherly affection, and brotherly affection with love. —RSV

Questions for Discussion:

1. How do you define love?

2. Where does love come from?

3. What are some of the implications for you as a Christian?

4. Would you say you are a loving person?

5. What things interfere with our being loving people, 24/7?

6. Do you spend more time hoarding love or sharing love through your actions?

7. How can you better let your love show through at work?

8. How important is consistency, over time, for instilling belief in your sincerity?

Study Session 5

Faith Trumps Law

Verses quoted in chapter 2, beginning with section titled "Love for All":

Romans 2:11.
For God does not show favoritism.

John 3:16.
For God so loved the world that he gave his one and only Son, that whoever believes in him shall not perish but have eternal life.

Galatians 2:16.
Know that a man is not justified by observing the law, but by faith in Jesus Christ. So we, too, have put our faith in Christ Jesus that we may be justified by faith in Christ and not by observing the law, because by observing the law no one will be justified.

It is important to note that while only a couple paragraphs of the book deal with the subject of faith trumping law as the path to salvation, the implications of this concept are foundational to Christianity. Therefore, you'll find the concept is broadly woven throughout the New Testament.

Central to the discussion is the fact that Jesus Christ became the path to salvation for all of us when he took the sins of mankind upon himself and was crucified on our behalf. Additionally, the love he expressed through that act is the source of the love that is in us and by letting it have continued expression through us we live our lives as intended by God.

Merely following the dictates of the laws established prior to the coming of Christ does not fulfill our purpose, nor gain us salvation. In effect, the law was put forth prior to Jesus' coming, so we could better appreciate our propensity for sin and our inability to achieve redemption on our own. We all fall short of being able to abide by 100 percent of the laws, 100 percent of the time.

Through recognition of our sinful nature, we can now better appreciate the necessity of Jesus' sacrifice. We know we are incapable of building a bridge of redemption that spans the gap between our imperfect nature and God's kingdom; thus, we rest our hope of gaining salvation on our belief in Jesus Christ as our Lord and Savior. He is our bridge.

God's Impartial Nature

Acts 10:28.
God has shown me that I should not call any man common or unclean.

Acts 10:34–35.
Then Peter began to speak: "I now realize how true it is that God does not show favoritism but accepts men from every nation who fear him and do what is right."

Romans 10:11.
As the Scripture says, "Anyone who trusts in him will never be put to shame."

John 20:30–31.
Jesus did many other miraculous signs in the presence of his disciples, which are not recorded in this book. But these are written that you may believe that Jesus is the Christ, the Son of God, and that by believing you may have life in his name.

Titus 2:11.
For the grace of God that brings salvation has appeared to all men.

Jesus Came to Save Sinners

Matthew 9:11–12.
When the Pharisees saw this, they asked his disciples, "Why does your teacher eat with tax collectors and 'sinners'?" On hearing this, Jesus said, "It is not the healthy who need a doctor, but the sick."

Mark 2:17.
I have not come to call the righteous, but sinners.

New Covenant Established through Jesus's Sacrifice

2 Corinthians 3:5–6.
Not that we are competent in ourselves to claim anything for ourselves, but our competence comes from God. He has made us competent as ministers of a new covenant—not of the letter but of the Spirit; for the letter kills, but the Spirit gives life.

Romans 8:2.
Because through Christ Jesus the law of the Spirit of life set me free from the law of sin and death.

Matthew 26:26–28.
While they were eating, Jesus took bread, gave thanks and broke it, and gave it to his disciples, saying, "Take and eat; this is my body." Then he took the cup, gave thanks and offered it to them, saying, "Drink from it, all of you. This is my blood of the covenant, which is poured out for many for the forgiveness of sins."

1 Peter 1:18–19.
For you know that it was not with perishable things such as silver or gold that you were redeemed from the empty way of life handed down to you from your forefathers, but with the precious blood of Christ, a lamb without blemish or defect.

Salvation Is Gained through Faith, Not Works of the Law

Romans 1:17.
The righteous will live by faith.

Romans 3:28.
For we maintain that a man is justified by faith apart from observing the law.

Romans 4:13.
It was not through law that Abraham and his offspring received the promise that he would be heir of the world, but through the righteousness that comes by faith.

Romans 7:6.
But now, by dying to what once bound us, we have been released from the law so that we serve in the new way of the Spirit, and not in the old way of the written code.

John 1:17.
For the law was given through Moses; grace and truth came through Jesus Christ.

Acts 13:38–39.
Therefore, my brothers, I want you to know that through Jesus the forgiveness of sins is proclaimed to you. Through him everyone who believes is justified from everything you could not be justified from by the law of Moses.

Galatians 2:21.
I do not set aside the grace of God, for if righteousness could be gained through the law, Christ died for nothing!

Romans 10:4.
Christ is the end of the law so that there may be righteousness for everyone who believes.

Hebrews 7:28.
For the law appoints as high priests men who are weak; but the oath, which came after the law, appointed the Son, who has been made perfect forever.

Luke 7:50.
Jesus said to the woman, "Your faith has saved you; go in peace."

The Law Exists to Make Our Imperfect Nature Evident

Romans 7:7.
Yet, if it had not been for the law, I should not have known sin. I should not have known what it is to covet if the law had not said, "You shall not covet."

John 8:7.
If any one of you is without sin, let him be the first to throw a stone at her.

Romans 5:20–21.
The law was added so that the trespass might increase. But where sin increased, grace increased all the more, so that, just as sin reigned in death, so also grace might reign through righteousness to bring eternal life through Jesus Christ our Lord.

Galatians 3:24.
So the law was put in charge to lead us to Christ that we might be justified by faith.

Focus on Sharing God's Love, and You'll Fulfill the Law

Galatians 5:14.
The entire law is summed up in a single command: "Love thy neighbor as yourself."
—NLT

Romans: 13:10.
Love does no wrong to others, so love fulfills the requirements of God's law.
—NLT

See also: Galatians chapters 3 and 4—By Faith, Not Works, and The Purpose of Law.

Questions for Discussion:

1. How is faith in receiving God's grace through Jesus more inclusive than adherence to the laws found in the Old Testament?

2. Why is salvation through faith (not deeds) an important concept for Christianity?

3. Which better describes you: someone who tries to do the right thing or someone who lives according to his or her faith?

4. What does living a life led by faith look like?

5. Do you need to make any changes in your approach to life to make your faith central to your motivations and resolve?

6. Can you act out of love for everyone?

7. Who do you work with that you need to consciously remind yourself to be more loving toward?

Study Session 6

All Christians Are Called to Be Leaders

Verse quoted in first half of chapter 3:

Matthew 5:14–16.
You are the light of the world. A city on a hill cannot be hidden. Neither do people light a lamp and put it under a bowl. Instead they put it on its stand, and it gives light to everyone in the house. In the same way, let your light shine before men, that they may see your good deeds and praise your Father in heaven.

By staying true to the faith that leads us and allowing it to power our actions and words, we naturally emit God's love so others can come to know and praise his glory. In effect, we are shining a light in the darkness of the world to help others find their way back to God. And if you have ever walked from darkness into a lighted room, you know that no matter how small the source, light always conquers darkness.

As long as Christians walk in the light that emanates from within themselves, those around them will also enjoy the blessings of God's love. All that is required is that you just allow yourself to be yourself—someone who is fueled by faith!

So remember to keep the light on and the door open when you head to work, and by keeping the darkness from gaining ground in a major part of your life, you also will provide others with the means to see and appreciate the invitation to experience God's majesty and grace.

Called to Bear Fruit

John 12:46.
I have come into the world as a light, so that no one who believes in me should stay in darkness.

Romans 13:12.
The night is nearly over; the day is almost here. So let us put aside the deeds of darkness and put on the armor of light.

Luke 11:36.
Therefore, if your whole body is full of light, and no part of it dark, it will be completely lighted, as when the light of a lamp shines on you.

Acts 13:47. "I have made you a light for the Gentiles, that you may bring salvation to the ends of the earth."

2 Timothy 4:5.
But you, keep your head in all situations, endure hardship, do the work of an evangelist, discharge all the duties of your ministry.

Ephesians 5:8–10.
For once you were darkness, but now you are light in the Lord; walk as children of light (for the fruit of light is found in all that is good and right and true), and try to learn what is pleasing to the Lord. —RSV

Galatians 5:22–23.
But the fruit of the Spirit is love, joy, peace, patience, kindness, goodness, faithfulness, gentleness and self-control. Against such things there is no law.

God Works through Us to Reach Others

Matthew 9:37–38.
"The harvest is plentiful but the workers are few. Ask the Lord of the harvest, therefore, to send out workers into his harvest field."

2 Thessalonians 1:11–12.
To this end we always pray for you, that our God may make

you worthy of his call, and may fulfill every good resolve and work of faith by his power, so that the name of our Lord Jesus may be glorified in you, and you in him, according to the grace of our God and the Lord Jesus Christ. —RSV

James 5:20.
Remember this: Whoever turns a sinner from the error of his way will save him from death and cover over a multitude of sins.

2 Corinthians 5:14–15.
For Christ's love compels us, because we are convinced that one died for all, and therefore all died. And he died for all, that those who live should no longer live for themselves but for him who died for them and was raised again.

Philippians 3:14-16.
I press on toward the goal to win the prize for which God has called me heavenward in Christ Jesus. All of us who are mature should take such a view of things. And if on some point you think differently, that too God will make clear to you. Only let us live up to what we have already attained.

See also: Hebrews chapter 11—Examples of Faith

Questions for Discussion:

1. How bright is your light?

2. What can you do to further strengthen your faith?

3. How is being true to your faith different from expecting others to adopt your beliefs and values?

4. How can you better let your faith shine through at work?

5. What is a specific example of something new that you will do this week to let God work through you?

Study Session 7

Faith Is an Active State

Verses quoted in chapter 3, beginning with the section "Belief Starts inside You":

Luke 6:45.
The good man brings good things out of the good stored up in his heart, and the evil man brings evil things out of the evil stored up in his heart. For out of the overflow of his heart his mouth speaks.

James 2:19, 26.
You believe that there is one God. Good! Even the demons believe that—and shudder ... As the body without the spirit is dead, so faith without deeds is dead.

John 7:21–25.
So I find this law at work: Although I want to do good, evil is right there with me. For in my inner being I delight in God's law; but I see another law at work in me, waging war against the law of my mind and making me a prisoner of the law of sin at work within me. What a wretched man I am! Who will rescue me from this body that is subject to death? Thanks be to God, who delivers me through Jesus Christ our Lord!

Romans 11:32.
For God has bound everyone over to disobedience so that he may have mercy on them all.

John 13:17.
Now that you know these things, you will be blessed if you do them.

Galatians 5:9.
A little yeast works through the whole batch of dough.

Mark 4:30–32.
Again he said, "What shall we say the kingdom of God is like, or what parable shall we use to describe it? It is like a mustard seed, which is the smallest seed you plant in the ground. Yet when planted, it grows and becomes the largest of all garden plants, with such big branches that the birds of the air can perch in its shade."

Ephesians 3:16–21.
I pray that out of his glorious riches he may strengthen you with power through his Spirit in your inner being, so that Christ may dwell in your hearts through faith. And I pray that you, being rooted and established in love, may have power, together with all the saints, to grasp how wide and long and high and deep is the love of Christ, and to know this love that surpasses knowledge—that you may be filled to the measure of all the fullness of God.

Now to him who is able to do immeasurably more than all we ask or imagine, according to his power that is at work within us, to him be glory in the church and in Christ Jesus throughout all generations, for ever and ever! Amen.

Actions speak louder than words, because actions require internal motivation and therefore are more likely to represent what you really value and believe. When someone says he will do something for you by a certain day but he fails to meet his commitment, he risks losing credibility with you the next time he makes a similar offer. The same holds true with faith.

When you say you believe in the truth of God's Word and in Jesus as Lord and Savior, the expectation is that your belief will lead to behaviors that reflect that commitment. Granted, we will all come up short of being perfect in all we do. We will still make poor choices due to our fallible natures. We also will vary in the areas that we individually emphasize as an expression of our faith. That is all part of being unique contributors to God's overall plan.

The point is that we need to park our fear of falling short of our commitment—accept that we will—and focus more on the strength our faith provides us to move forward. Count on your faith for guidance, and you'll find the inspiration to try. Every little bit counts, and with conscious practice it should become habit. Putting forth more of what is right will always be better than never sharing it all.

Belief Begets Response

John 14:12.
I tell you the truth, anyone who has faith in me will do what I have been doing ...

James 2:14.
What good is it, my brothers, if a man claims to have faith but has no deeds? Can such faith save him?

James 2:26.
As the body without the spirit is dead, so faith without deeds is dead.

Called to Move Forward

John 10:27.
My sheep hear My voice, and I know them, and they follow Me.

Luke 9:62.
Jesus replied, "No one who puts his hand to the plow and looks back is fit for service in the kingdom of God."

Luke 3:8.
Prove by the way you live that you have repented of your sins and turned to God ...

James 1:22.
Do not merely listen to the word, and so deceive yourselves. Do what it says.

1 John 3:18.
Dear children, let us not love with words or tongue but with actions and in truth.

Every Little Bit Helps

Matthew 13:33.
He told them still another parable: "The kingdom of heaven is like yeast that a woman took and mixed into a large amount of flour until it worked all through the dough."

Questions for Discussion:

1. Is faith meant to be passive or active?

_____

2. Why is this important?

_____

3. How active is your faith?

_____

4. Where is your faith most active in your life?

_____

5. How can you better integrate your faith into your job?

_____

6. What is one small thing you can change in your routine at work to better reflect your faith?

_____

Part II
Inspired Behavior

Maintain shared purpose.

Study Session 8:

Servant Leadership

Verses quoted in the first half of chapter 4:

Luke 22:26.
But among you it will be different. Those who are the greatest among you should take the lowest rank, and the leader should be like a servant. —NLT

Matthew 20:26–28.
Whoever wants to become great among you must be your servant, and whoever wants to be first must be your slave— just as the Son of Man did not come to be served, but to serve, and to give his life as a ransom for many.

1 Timothy 6:17–19.
Command those who are rich in this present world not to be arrogant nor to put their hope in wealth, which is so uncertain, but to put their hope in God, who richly provides us with everything for our enjoyment. Command them to do good, to be rich in good deeds, and to be generous and willing to share. In this way they will lay up treasure for themselves as a firm foundation for the coming age, so that they may take hold of the life that is truly life.

James 3:16–17.
For where you have envy and selfish ambition, there you find disorder and every evil practice. But the wisdom that comes from heaven is first of all pure; then peace-loving, considerate, submissive, full of mercy and good fruit, impartial and sincere.

The Bible provides many powerful leadership examples that allow us to see that elements of faith are the reasons why the leaders of the Bible chose their respective paths and endured their personal challenges. Through them, we find that building our own deeply held faith is of primary importance in order to find the proper inspiration and resolve to confidently pursue the correct course of action in any situation we face. Inspired actions follow deeply held values and beliefs, not vice versa.

Always remember that behaviors are not the goal; they are the result. Look at yourself through the eyes of an objective doctor, and think of your actions as visible symptoms that help you diagnose the health of your underlying faith.

Because actions arise from belief, the need for a strong basis in faith has been the emphasis in our study up until this point. Now, the remainder of this study guide will provide a few examples of broad behaviors you may expect to see from a leader who finds their motivation in their faith.

How does a Christian leader appear to others? To begin with, all Christians are called to be servant leaders, with Jesus Christ as their role model.

Servant leadership is the natural outcome of sharing God's love. It requires willingly and joyfully putting the interests of others ahead of our own desires and adopting a definition of personal success that is less about the stuff we accumulate and more about how we use what we have been given—talent, money, authority, time, empathy—to benefit others.

With that in mind, let's strive to accomplish three things as we reflect on the verses and questions in this study session:

1. Recognize that servant leadership is the outcome of a well-developed Christian faith.
2. Raise awareness of areas in our lives where we can establish guardrails to halt the erosion of our calling.
3. Establish some momentum that helps us mature as servant leaders.

Anchoring ourselves in our respective situations today and establishing momentum for better reflecting our values and beliefs through our behaviors is a worthy starting point from which we can all build through continued study, counsel, and prayer. Today, let's get the ball rolling in the right direction!

The following verses are but a few of those found in the Bible that provide a view of what real success looks like for a servant leader, as well as some of the hurdles we have to overcome to live our lives as God intends.

Serve as He Served

Mark 9:35.
Sitting down, Jesus called the Twelve and said, "If anyone wants to be first, he must be the very last, and the servant of all."

John 13:14.
Now that I, your Lord and Teacher, have washed your feet, you also should wash one another's feet.

Matthew 23:11–12.
The greatest among you will be your servant. For whoever exalts himself will be humbled, and whoever humbles himself will be exalted.

1 Corinthians 10:24.
Nobody should seek his own good, but the good of others.

Success Is More than More Stuff

I Timothy 6:10.
For the love of money is a root of all kinds of evil. Some people, eager for money, have wandered from the faith and pierced themselves with many griefs.

Luke 16:13.
No servant can serve two masters. Either he will hate the one and love the other, or he will be devoted to the one and despise the other. You cannot serve both God and Money.

Matthew 6:21.
For where your treasure is, there your heart will be also.

Matthew 19:24–26.
"Again I tell you, it is easier for a camel to go through the eye of a needle than for a rich man to enter the kingdom of God." When the disciples heard this, they were greatly astonished and asked, "Who then can be saved?" Jesus looked at them

and said, "With man this is impossible, but with God all things are possible."

Hebrews 13:5.
Keep your life free from love of money, and be content with what you have; for he has said, "I will never fail you nor forsake you." —RSV

1 Timothy 6:6–8.
But godliness with contentment is great gain. For we brought nothing into the world, and we can take nothing out of it. But if we have food and clothing, we will be content with that.

Remember We Are Only Stewards of What God Provides Us

Romans 11:36.
For from him and through him and to him are all things. To him be the glory forever! Amen.

Luke 16:10–12.
Whoever can be trusted with very little can also be trusted with much, and whoever is dishonest with very little will also be dishonest with much. So if you have not been trustworthy in handling worldly wealth, who will trust you with true riches? And if you have not been trustworthy with someone else's property, who will give you property of your own?

1 Peter 4:8–10.
Above all, love each other deeply, because love covers over a multitude of sins. Offer hospitality to one another without grumbling. Each of you should use whatever gift you have received to serve others, as faithful stewards of God's grace in its various forms.

Serving Implies Giving, Not Hoarding

Acts 20:35.
"It is more blessed to give than to receive."

Luke 3:11.
John answered, "The man with two tunics should share with

him who has none, and the one who has food should do the same."

1 John 3:17.
If anyone has material possessions and sees his brother in need but has no pity on him, how can the love of God be in him?

Luke 9:25.
What good is it for a man to gain the whole world, and yet lose or forfeit his very self?

2 Corinthians 8:13–14.
Our desire is not that others might be relieved while you are hard pressed, but that there might be equality. At the present time your plenty will supply what they need, so that in turn their plenty will supply what you need. The goal is equality.

2 Corinthians 9:7.
Each man should give what he has decided in his heart to give, not reluctantly or under compulsion, for God loves a cheerful giver.

See also: Luke 10:25–37, the story of the Good Samaritan; and 2 Corinthians 8–9, The Cheerful Giver.

Questions for Discussion:

1. How is servant leadership a natural result of faith?

2. How much is eternal salvation worth?

3. How much does it cost?

4. What acts would you expect to see from the faithfully rich?

5. How much financial wealth is enough?

6. How does love of money show up in your life?

7. What are some examples of how external influences make you want more money or stuff when your internal faith is saying you have more than enough?

8. Other than money, what resources has God put in your stewardship?

9. How will you allow yourself to be more expressive of God's love with the resources and skills with which you've been entrusted?

10. What are two goals you can set for yourself at work this week that will measurably demonstrate your performance as a servant leader?

Study Session 9

Strength in Weakness

Verses quoted in chapter 4, beginning with the section "Cultural Implication: Need to Redefine Strength":

Colossians 3:12–14.
Therefore, as God's chosen people, holy and dearly loved, clothe yourselves with compassion, kindness, humility, gentleness and patience. Bear with each other and forgive whatever grievances you may have against one another. Forgive as the Lord forgave you. And over all these virtues put on love, which binds them all together in perfect unity.

2 Corinthians 13:4.
Although he was crucified in weakness, he now lives by the power of God … —NLT

2 Timothy 1:7.
For God did not give us a spirit of timidity, but a spirit of power, of love, and of self-discipline.

The concept of purposely embracing vulnerability can be a scary idea. It is not easy to accept that we are not in control and even harder to knowingly do things that accentuate that fact.

As servant leaders, Christians embrace vulnerability and humility because they are emboldened by God's power and love and the hope of eternal salvation through Jesus Christ. By believing in the truth of God's Word, the outward appearance of their faith is self-fulfilling.

The challenge is to recognize that the upsides that come from accepting God's plan for our life far exceed what we can achieve by exercising our own power. Trusting God is a requisite part of believing, so let go and enjoy the ride!

Strength Redefined

1 Corinthians 3:18–19.
Do not deceive yourselves. If any one of you thinks he is wise by the standards of this age, he should become a "fool" so that he may become wise. For the wisdom of this world is foolishness in God's sight. As it is written: "He catches the wise in their craftiness."

1 Corinthians 1:27–29.
But God chose the foolish things of the world to shame the wise; God chose the weak things of the world to shame the strong. He chose the lowly things of this world and the despised things—and the things that are not—to nullify the things that are, so that no one may boast before him.

Philippians 4:5.
Let your gentleness be evident to all. The Lord is near.

2 Timothy 2:1.
You then, my son, be strong in the grace that is in Christ Jesus.

2 Corinthians 12:9.
My grace is sufficient for you, for my power is made perfect in weakness …

Luke 17:33.
Whoever tries to keep his life will lose it, and whoever loses his life will preserve it.

Act Out of Humility, Not Pride

Philippians 2:3.
Do nothing out of selfish ambition or vain conceit, but in humility consider others better than yourselves.

1 Corinthians 1:31.
Let him who boasts, boast of the Lord.

1 Peter 5:5.
All of you, clothe yourselves with humility toward one another, because, "God opposes the proud but gives grace to the humble."

James 4:10.
Humble yourselves before the Lord, and he will lift you up.

Matthew 18:4.
Therefore, whoever humbles himself like this child is the greatest in the kingdom of heaven.

See also: Matthew 5:1–10, excerpt from the Sermon on the Mount.

Questions for Discussion:

1. What strengths do you need to succeed in your line of work?

2. What do the strengths you listed imply about how you define professional success?

3. What are the strengths of a faithful Christian?

4. Is your definition of success at work supportive of or in conflict with the overall purpose God has defined for your life?

5. One year from now, how would you want people to describe your strengths?

6. What can you do this week to begin exhibiting those strengths?

Study Session 10

One Community

Verses quoted in chapter 5 of the book:

Romans 12:4–5.
For as in one body we have many members, and all the members do not have the same function, so we, though many, are one body in Christ, and individually members one of another. —RSV

Ecclesiastes 4:9–10.
Two are better than one, because they have a nice return for their work: If one falls down, his friend can help him up. But pity the man who falls and has no one to help him up!

1 Peter 4:10.
As each has received a gift, employ it for one another, as good stewards of God's varied grace. —RSV

1 Corinthians 12:24–26.
But God has so composed the body, giving the greater honor to the inferior part, that there may be no discord in the body, but that the members may have the same care for one another. If one member suffers, all suffer together; if one member is honored, all rejoice together. —RSV

Romans 12:10.
Love each other with genuine affection, and take delight in honoring each other. —NLT

We are all meant to be inextricably linked together as complementary contributors to the community of Christ, in whom we find the bond that gives us shared purpose and fellowship. With Jesus central to our being, the glue that binds us is that of the servant leader, found in our expression of his compassion, empathy, joy, and love for one another.

The metaphor of one body with many complementary parts makes clear the collective power of community and the futility of being a lone contributor. The body regrets the loss of any member but can find consolation and support from its remaining parts. The lost member, however, is not so fortunate. Luckily, what is lost in human terms can still be found and rejoined to the community.

Likewise, individuals who join in the body of Christ are intended to become linked to the broader community to maximize their potential and provide them with support. Enjoy the fact that you can find more fulfillment as part of a larger entity than yourself. A thumb is just a thumb until it is part of a hand.

Embrace Community and Fellowship

1 John 1:3.
We proclaim to you what we have seen and heard, so that you also may have fellowship with us. And our fellowship is with the Father and with his Son, Jesus Christ.

1 Corinthians 1:9.
God, who has called you into fellowship with his Son Jesus Christ our Lord, is faithful.

1 John 1:7.
But if we walk in the light, as he is in the light, we have fellowship with one another, and the blood of Jesus, his Son, purifies us from all sin.

We Are All in This Together

John 17:11.
I will remain in the world no longer, but they are still in the world, and I am coming to you. Holy Father, protect them by the power of your name—the name you gave me—so that they may be one as we are one.

Colossians 3:15.
Let the peace of Christ rule in your hearts, since as members of one body you were called to peace. And be thankful.

1 Corinthians 3:8–9.
The man who plants and the man who waters have one purpose, and each will be rewarded according to his own labor. For we are God's fellow workers; you are God's field, God's building.

1 Corinthians 12:20.
As it is, there are many parts, but one body.

1 Corinthians 12:27.
Now you are the body of Christ, and each one of you is a part of it.

Acts 2:44.
All the believers were together and had everything in common.

Romans 14:7.
For none of us lives to himself alone and none of us dies to himself alone.

Many Hands Make Light the Load

Galatians 6:2.
Carry one another's burdens, and in this way you will fulfill the law of Christ.

1 Corinthians 10:24.
Nobody should seek his own good, but the good of others.

Philippians 2:4.
Each of you should look not only to your own interests, but also to the interests of others.

Everyone Has the Ability to Contribute

I Corinthians 7:7.
I wish that all men were as I am. But each man has his own gift from God; one has this gift, another has that.

1 Corinthians 12:4–6.
There are different kinds of gifts, but the same Spirit distributes them. There are different kinds of service, but the same Lord. There are different kinds of working, but in all of them and in everyone it is the same God at work.

Romans 12:6.
Having gifts that differ according to grace given to us, let us use them. —RSV

Build Up Your Co-workers

Romans 14:19.
So then, let us aim for harmony in the church and try to build each other up. —NLT

1 Thessalonians 5:11.
Therefore encourage one another and build each other up, just as in fact you are doing.

Romans 1:12.
That is, that you and I may be mutually encouraged by each other's faith.

Questions for Discussion:

1. How does being part of a community differ from belonging to a team?

2. What are the elements of a well-functioning community?

3. How does your work environment compare to your definition of community?

4. How can you contribute to building a stronger sense of community at your place of employment?

5. With whom can you improve your relationship to positively impact your job?

6. What steps can you take to improve that relationship?

Study Session 11

Good Communities Communicate

Verses quoted in chapter 6 of the book:

James 3:2.
Indeed we all make mistakes. For if we could control our tongues, we would be perfect and could also control ourselves in every other way. —NLT

Ephesians 4:29.
Do not let any unwholesome talk come out of your mouths, but only what is helpful for building others up according to their needs, that it may benefit those who listen.

2 Timothy 2:23–26.
Don't have anything to do with foolish and stupid arguments, because you know they produce quarrels. And the Lord's servant must not quarrel; instead, he must be kind to everyone, able to teach, not resentful. Those who oppose him he must gently instruct, in the hope that God will grant them repentance leading them to a knowledge of the truth, and that they will come to their senses and escape from the trap of the devil, who has taken them captive to do his will.

James 1:19.
Everyone should be quick to listen, slow to speak and slow to become angry.

Matthew 18:15–16.
If your brother sins against you, go and show him his fault, just between the two of you. If he listens to you, you have won

your brother over. But if he will not listen, take one or two others along, so that "every matter may be established by the testimony of two or three witnesses."

1 Peter 2:1.
Therefore, rid yourselves of all malice and all deceit, hypocrisy, envy, and slander of every kind.

Everything is a form of communication, especially our words. How we say something and what we actually say speak volumes of the source within us—whether we act out of selfish motivation, blind response, or loving intent.

As the verses above and below point out, the Bible provides good advice to keep our communication constructive. It all begins with staying consistent with our internal Christian values and beliefs that keep love central to the conversation.

Speak Out of Positive Motivation

Ephesians 4:15.
Instead, we will speak the truth in love, growing in every way more and more like Christ, who is the head of his body, the church. —NLT

Titus 3:2.
To slander no one, to be peaceable and considerate, and to show true humility toward all men.

Galatians 5:25–26.
Since we live by the Spirit, let us keep in step with the Spirit. Let us not become conceited, provoking and envying each other.

1 Peter 3:15–17.
But in your hearts set apart Christ as Lord. Always be prepared to give an answer to everyone who asks you to give the reason for the hope that you have. But do this with gentleness and respect, keeping a clear conscience, so that those who speak maliciously against your good behavior in Christ may be ashamed of their slander. It is better, if it is God's will, to suffer for doing good than for doing evil.

Avoid Senseless Arguments

Titus 3:9.
But avoid foolish controversies and genealogies and arguments and quarrels about the law, because these are unprofitable and useless.

James 1:26.
If anyone considers himself religious and yet does not keep a tight rein on his tongue, he deceives himself and his religion is worthless.

2 Timothy 2:14–16.
Keep reminding them of these things. Warn them before God against quarreling about words; it is of no value, and only ruins those who listen. Do your best to present yourself to God as one approved, a workman who does not need to be ashamed and who correctly handles the word of truth. Avoid godless chatter, because those who indulge in it will become more and more ungodly.

And Control Your Tongue

James 3:5. Likewise the tongue is a small part of the body, but it makes great boasts. Consider what a great forest is set on fire by a small spark.

1 Peter 3:10.
For, "Whoever would love life and see good days must keep his tongue from evil and his lips from deceitful speech."

Ephesians 4:31–32.
Get rid of all bitterness, rage and anger, brawling and slander, along with every form of malice. Be kind and compassionate to one another, forgiving each other, just as in Christ God forgave you.

Questions for Discussion:

1. What are some of your biggest communication challenges at work?

2. Which of the verses in this section resonate most with you, and why?

3. Is there one verse in particular that you feel offers great advice to you?

4. What improvements do you expect to see over the next week as a result of applying the verses above? Over the next six months?

Study Session 12

Hope and Endurance

Verses quoted in chapter 7 of the book:

Hebrews 10:23–24.
Let us hold unswervingly to the hope we profess, for he who promised is faithful. And let us consider how we may spur one another on toward love and good deeds.

Romans 5:3–5.
More than that, we rejoice in our sufferings, knowing that suffering produces endurance and endurance produces character, and character produces hope, and hope does not disappoint us, because God's love has been poured into our hearts through the Holy Spirit which has been given to us.

Hebrews 10:36.
Patient endurance is what you need now, so that you will continue to do God's will. Then you will receive all that he has promised. —NLT

1 Peter 2:18.
Servants, be submissive to your masters with all respect, not only to the kind but also to the overbearing. —RSV

1 Peter 1:6–7.
So be truly glad. There is wonderful joy ahead, even though you have to endure many trials for a little while. These trials will show that your faith is genuine. It is being tested as fire tests and purifies gold—though your faith is far more precious than mere gold. So when your faith remains strong through

many trials, it will bring you much praise and glory and honor on the day when Jesus Christ is revealed to the whole world.
—NLT

Humans regularly demonstrate the internal fortitude to resist nagging addictions, follow restrictive diets, perform heroic feats, and survive extreme hardships. Sometimes they succeed because they fear negative consequences if they fail, but mostly they succeed because they find motivation in their sense of purpose and hope.

Similarly, as Christians we find motivation in our faith and recognize that everything that occurs to us in this world has to happen as part of our journey. Celebrate each challenge and reward you receive for what it is—another mile marker passed on the path you have chosen. Always remember to keep your eyes on the prize you seek.

Find Resolve in Your Faith

Luke 9:23.
Then he said to them all: "If anyone would come after me, he must deny himself and take up his cross daily and follow me."

2 Timothy 2:3–4.
Endure hardship with us like a good soldier of Christ Jesus. No one serving as a soldier gets involved in civilian affairs—he wants to please his commanding officer.

Romans 5:1–2.
Therefore, since we have been justified through faith, we have peace with God through our Lord Jesus Christ, through whom we have gained access by faith into this grace in which we now stand. And we rejoice in the hope of the glory of God.

2 Peter 3:13.
But in keeping with his promise we are looking forward to a new heaven and a new earth, the home of righteousness.

John 16:33.
I have told you these things, so that in me you may have peace.

In this world you will have trouble. But take heart! I have overcome the world.

Submit to Worldly Authorities, But Hold True to Your Faith

Romans 13:1.
Everyone must submit himself to the governing authorities, for there is no authority except that which God has established. The authorities that exist have been established by God.

1 Peter 4:19.
Therefore let those who suffer according to God's will do right and entrust their souls to a faithful Creator. —RSV

1 Timothy 6:1.
All who are under the yoke of slavery should consider their masters worthy of full respect, so that God's name and our teaching may not be slandered.

Titus 3:1.
Remind them to be submissive to rulers and authorities, to be obedient and ready for any honest work. —RSV

Matthew 22:21.
Give to Caesar what is Caesar's, and to God what is God's.

1 Peter 2:13–15.
Submit yourselves for the Lord's sake to every authority instituted among men: whether to the king, as the supreme authority, or to governors, who are sent by him to punish those who do wrong and to commend those who do right. For it is God's will that by doing good you should silence the ignorant talk of foolish men.

Perseverance Is Part of the Plan

James 5:11.
As you know, we consider blessed those who have persevered. You have heard of Job's perseverance and have seen what the Lord finally brought about. The Lord is full of compassion and mercy.

2 Corinthians 12:10.
That is why, for Christ's sake, I delight in weaknesses, in insults, in hardships, in persecutions, in difficulties. For when I am weak, then I am strong.

James 1:2–4.
Consider it pure joy, my brothers, whenever you face trials of many kinds, ³because you know that the testing of your faith develops perseverance. ⁴Perseverance must finish its work so that you may be mature and complete, not lacking anything.

Romans 5:3–5.
Not only so, but we also rejoice in our sufferings, because we know that suffering produces perseverance; perseverance, character; and character, hope. And hope does not disappoint us, because God has poured out his love into our hearts by the Holy Spirit, whom he has given us.

Romans 8:18.
I consider that our present sufferings are not worth comparing with the glory that will be revealed in us.

Endurance Reflects Your Faith

James 1:12. Blessed is the man who perseveres under trial, because when he has stood the test, he will receive the crown of life that God has promised to those who love him.

Matthew 5:10.
Blessed are those who are persecuted because of righteousness, for theirs is the kingdom of heaven.

Luke 21:19.
By your endurance you will gain your lives. —RSV

1 Peter 4:19.
So then, those who suffer according to God's will should commit themselves to their faithful Creator and continue to do good.

2 Timothy 4:7.
I have fought the good fight, I have finished the race, I have kept the faith.

Servant Leaders Endure to Benefit Others

Hebrews 12:3–4.
Consider him who endured such opposition from sinful men, so that you will not grow weary and lose heart. In your struggle against sin, you have not yet resisted to the point of shedding your blood.

John 10:11.
I am the good shepherd. The good shepherd lays down his life for the sheep.

John 15:13.
Greater love has no one than this, that he lay down his life for his friends.

Questions for Discussion:

1. What are some of the most recurrent challenges to your faith that you have to face?

2. How does a strong faith help you to overcome obstacles you may encounter?

3. How does the hope of salvation provide an anchor to pull you through life's adversities?

4. What is the benefit of knowing your work is subordinate to your overall purpose in life?

5. Do you feel your internal commitment to living your faith is getting stronger, weaker, or holding steady?

6. What does successfully reinforcing your faith look like if you picture yourself one year from now?

7. What is a recent adversity you have faced? Can you thank God for how it affected you or someone else?

8. Who can you rely on to support your growth going forward?

Born Anew

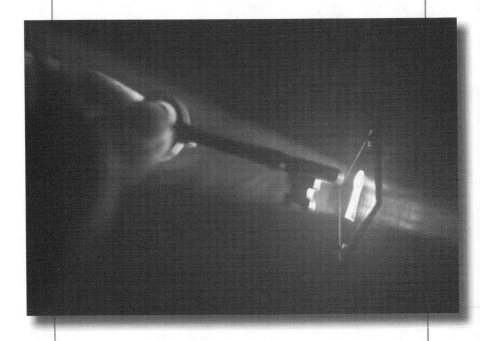

Use your key

Final Study Session:

Baptism and the Holy Spirit

Verse quoted in the afterword:

> Romans 6:3–4.
> Or have you forgotten that when we were joined with Christ
> Jesus in baptism, we joined him in his death? For we died and
> were buried with Christ by baptism. And just as Christ was
> raised from the dead by the glorious power of the Father, now
> we also may live new lives. —NLT

From the Scriptures referenced in earlier study sessions, we know
that good deeds and servant leadership are the natural outpourings of a
Christian's faith. Our actions reflect our commitment.

Likewise, the act of being baptized signifies our acceptance of Jesus
Christ as our Lord and Savior and commitment to being reborn as a
member of the body of Christ. It is also the step that prepares us for
receiving the gift of the Holy Spirit, which acts as our counselor in the
truth, and reunites us with God through Jesus by linking us to the Holy
Trinity.

Those are very cursory highlights of the role of baptism and the Holy
Spirit, but God has kept it simple for us to help us make the right choice.
Salvation and eternal life are freely available to anyone who wants them.
We either believe or not believe. We can rely on his majesty and serve his
will, or we can seek to strike our own path. We can look to our faith for
our inspiration or choose to be led by worldly influences. In each case, the
options are clear, and the choice is ours to make.

Fortunately, God continually makes his good intentions and unyielding
love both visible and available, so we can enjoy his blessings. May we all

find it in us to join in the celebration of his glory by accepting the grace he gives us through Jesus Christ, our Lord and Savior.

Life Comes through Jesus Christ

John 1:1–5.
In the beginning was the Word, and the Word was with God, and the Word was God. He was in the beginning with God; all things were made through him, and without him was not anything made that was made. In him was life, and the life was the light of men. The light shines in the darkness, and the darkness has not overcome it.

John 5:39–40.
You diligently study the Scriptures because you think that by them you possess eternal life. These are the Scriptures that testify about me, yet you refuse to come to me to have life.

1 John 5:11–12.
And this is the testimony: God has given us eternal life, and this life is in his Son. He who has the Son has life; he who does not have the Son of God does not have life.

John 6:47–48.
Very truly I tell you, the one who believes has eternal life. I am the bread of life.

Revelations 22:17.
Let the one who is thirsty come; and let the one who wishes take the free gift of the water of life.

Jesus Is Our Bridge to Salvation

Mark 14:61–62.
But Jesus remained silent and gave no answer. Again the high priest asked him, "Are you the Christ, the Son of the Blessed One?" "I am," said Jesus. "And you will see the Son of Man sitting at the right hand of the Mighty One and coming on the clouds of heaven."

John 11:25–26.
Jesus said to her, "I am the resurrection and the life. He who

believes in me will live, even though he dies; and whoever lives and believes in me will never die. Do you believe this?"

John 8:24.
That is why I said that you will die in your sins; for unless you believe that I Aᴍ who I claim to be, you will die in your sins. —NLT

Romans 10:9.
That if you confess with your mouth, 'Jesus is Lord,' and believe in your heart that God raised him from the dead, you will be saved.

John 6:37–40.
All those the Father gives me will come to me, and whoever comes to me I will never drive away. For I have come down from heaven not to do my will but to do the will of him who sent me. And this is the will of him who sent me, that I shall lose none of all those he has given me, but raise them up at the last day. For my Father's will is that everyone who looks to the Son and believes in him shall have eternal life, and I will raise them up at the last day.

Galatians 3:11–13.
Clearly no one who relies on the law is justified before God, because "the righteous will live by faith." The law is not based on faith; on the contrary, it says, "The person who does these things will live by them." Christ redeemed us from the curse of the law by becoming a curse for us ...

Baptism Signals Our Conscious Commitment to Being Reborn

Ephesians 4:4–6.
There is one body and one Spirit, just as you were called to one hope when you were called; one Lord, one faith, one baptism; one God and Father of all, who is over all and through all and in all.

1 Peter 3:21–22.
And this water symbolizes baptism that now saves you also—not the removal of dirt from the body but the pledge of a clear

conscience toward God. It saves you by the resurrection of Jesus Christ, who has gone into heaven and is at God's right hand—with angels, authorities and powers in submission to him.

Acts 19:4–5.
Paul said, "John's baptism was a baptism of repentance. He told the people to believe in the one coming after him, that is, in Jesus." On hearing this, they were baptized in the name of the Lord Jesus.

And Prepares Us to Receive the Holy Spirit

Mark 1:6–8.
John wore clothing made of camel's hair, with a leather belt around his waist, and he ate locusts and wild honey. And this was his message: "After me comes the one more powerful than I, the straps of whose sandals I am not worthy to stoop down and untie. I baptize you with water, but he will baptize you with the Holy Spirit."

John 7:37–39.
On the last and greatest day of the festival, Jesus stood and said in a loud voice, "Let anyone who is thirsty come to me and drink. Whoever believes in me, as Scripture has said, rivers of living water will flow from within them." By this he meant the Spirit, whom those who believed in him were later to receive. Up to that time the Spirit had not been given, since Jesus had not yet been glorified.

John 3:5–7.
Jesus answered, "Truly, truly, I say to you, unless one is born of water and the Spirit, he cannot enter the kingdom of God. That which is born of the flesh is flesh, and that which is born of the Spirit, is spirit. Do not marvel that I said to you, 'You must be born anew.'"
—RSV

Acts 2:38.
Peter replied, "Repent and be baptized, every one of you, in

the name of Jesus Christ for the forgiveness of your sins. And you will receive the gift of the Holy Spirit."

The Holy Spirit Helps Us to Know the Truth

John 14:15–17.
If you love me, you will keep my commandments. And I will pray the Father, and he will give you another Counselor, to be with you for ever, even the Spirit of truth, whom the world cannot receive, because it neither sees him nor knows him; you know him, for he dwells with you and will be in you. —RSV

John 14:25–26.
These things I have spoken to you, while I am still with you. But the Counselor, the Holy Spirit, whom the Father will send in my name, he will teach you all things, and bring to your remembrance all that I have said to you. —RSV

1 John 5:6.
And it is the Spirit who testifies, because the Spirit is the truth.

1 Corinthians 2:12.
What we have received is not the spirit of the world, but the Spirit who is from God, so that we may understand what God has freely given us.

John 16:13.
When the Spirit of truth comes, he will guide you into all the truth.

And Reunites Us with God through Jesus Christ

John 10:30.
"I and the Father are one."

1 John 4:13–15.
This is how we know that we live in him and he in us: He has given us of his Spirit. And we have seen and testify that the Father has sent his Son to be the Savior of the world. If anyone

acknowledges that Jesus is the Son of God, God lives in them and they in God.

John 4:24.
God is spirit, and his worshipers must worship in the Spirit and in truth.

Romans 8:10–11, 14.
But if Christ is in you, then even though your body is subject to death because of sin, the Spirit gives life because of righteousness. And if the Spirit of him who raised Jesus from the dead is living in you, he who raised Christ from the dead will also give life to your mortal bodies because of his Spirit who lives in you. ... [14]For those who are led by the Spirit of God are the children of God.

Galatians 4:6.
Because you are his sons, God sent the Spirit of his Son into our hearts, the Spirit who calls out, "*Abba*, Father."

2 Corinthians 3:18.
And we all, who with unveiled faces contemplate the Lord's glory, are being transformed into his image with ever-increasing glory, which comes from the Lord, who is the Spirit.

2 Corinthians 5:17–19.
Therefore, if anyone is in Christ, the new creation has come: The old has gone, the new is here! All this is from God, who reconciled us to himself through Christ and gave us the ministry of reconciliation: that God was reconciling the world to himself in Christ, not counting people's sins against them. And he has committed to us the message of reconciliation.

Colossians 1:19–20.
For God was pleased to have all his fullness dwell in him, and through him to reconcile to himself all things, whether things on earth or things in heaven, by making peace through his blood, shed on the cross.

Titus 3:3–7.
At one time we too were foolish, disobedient, deceived and

enslaved by all kinds of passions and pleasures. We lived in malice and envy, being hated and hating one another. But when the kindness and love of God our Savior appeared, he saved us, not because of righteous things we had done, but because of his mercy. He saved us through the washing of rebirth and renewal by the Holy Spirit, whom he poured out on us generously through Jesus Christ our Savior, so that, having been justified by his grace, we might become heirs having the hope of eternal life.

John 14:20.
On that day you will realize that I am in my Father, and you are in me, and I am in you.

Questions for Discussion:

1. What stands out most from the study sessions you have completed?

   _____

2. What do you think has been placed on your heart to embrace or change as a result of your own reflections?

   _____

3. What steps can you take to make sure you continue moving toward fulfilling your purpose in life?

   _____

4. How do you plan to keep your faith in the forefront of your motivations?

   _____

5. Where does baptism fit in your growth plan?

   _____

6. With whom will you share your journey for mutual support?

   _____

7. What is the first step you will take this week to continue your journey?

   _____

Though our steps are simple, they are not easy. Road blocks and diversions abound to challenge our best intentions. Even so, the closer we get to what we are intended to be, the more clearly we find benefit, comfort, and peace, so perseverance has its rewards. With that in mind, I offer up the words of Paul as a concluding prayer for us all:

Hebrews 13:20–21.
May the God of peace, who through the blood of the eternal covenant brought back from the dead our Lord Jesus, that great Shepherd of the sheep, equip you with everything good for doing his will, and may he work in us what is pleasing to him, through Jesus Christ, to whom be glory for ever and ever. Amen.

Work hard.
Live well.
Amen.

About the Author

S cott Ortega is a senior marketing and sales executive, with over twenty years of demonstrated success in leadership positions with well-respected corporations, including the Sunrise Greetings Company, Diageo, and Frito-Lay, Inc. He also holds an MBA from Northwestern University, and a BA Finance and BS Marketing from the University of Utah.

Scott currently lives with his wife and youngest son in Sioux City, Iowa, where he continually strives to apply his new learning to his work on a daily basis.

Appendix A

Additional Resources

I. Author's website: www.Inspired-Work.com.

The following is a partial list of the materials and information you will find online at www.Inspired-Work.com:

- Brief synopsis of book's content.
- Links to social networking sites related to this book.
- Upcoming events.
- Media coverage..
- Access to useful tools for assessing individual personalities and strengths.

II. Focus on the Family's *The Truth Project* by Dr. Del Tackett.

This twelve-part series is available in DVD format and is designed specifically for use with small groups. I believe you will find it particularly useful for anchoring your belief in the universal truth found in God's Word.

For more information go to www.TheTruthProject.com.

References

- "Bosnian Serbs Jailed for Genocide." *News.BBC.co.uk*. July 29, 2008. Accessed April 28, 2011. http://news.bbc.co.uk/1/hi/world/europe/7531413.stm

- Carey, Anne R. and Paul Trap. "USA Today Snapshots." *USA Today*, April 20, 2011: 1A.

- Carson, Clayborne and Peter Holloran, eds. *A Knock at Midnight: Inspiration from the Great Sermons of Reverend Martin Luther King, Jr*. New York: Warner Books, 1998.

- Charny, Israel W., ed. *Encyclopedia of Genocide*. Volumes 1 and 2. Jerusalem: Institute on the Holocaust and Genocide, 1999.

- Dallaire, Romeo, and Brent Beardsley. *Shake Hands With The Devil: The Failure of Humanity in Rwanda*. Canada: Random House, 2003.

- Division of Christian Education of the National Council of the Churches of Christ in the United States of America, ed. *The Holy Bible*, Revised Standard Version. Nashville: Thomas Nelson, Inc. 1971.

- Kadlec, Dan. "How the Crisis is Changing You." *CNNMoney.com*, May 4, 2009. Accessed May 4, 2009. http://money.cnn.com/2009/05/01/pf/changing_values.moneymag/index.htm

- "Killing of Iraq Kurds 'Genocide'." *News.BBC.co.uk*. December 23, 2005. Accessed May 13, 2011. http://news.bbc.co.uk/2/hi/europe/4555000.stm

- "List of Countries by Percentage of Population Living Below the Poverty Line." *Wikipedia*. Access Date April 18, 2009. http://en.wikipedia.org/wiki/List_of_countries_by_percentage_of_population_living_in_poverty

- MacKenzie, Ross. "J.S. Bach: soli deo gloria." Soli Deo Gloria: Thoughts on Theology, Science, and Culture. May 28, 2009. Accessed May 13, 2011. http://revelation4-11.blogspot.com/2009/05/js-bach-soli-deo-gloria.html

- Mackinnon, Kevin. "Sucking the Marrow Out of Life." *Ironman. com.* February 13, 2006. Accessed May 13, 2011. http:// ironman.com/mediacenter/history/sucking-the-marrow-out-of-life#axzz1MG4296sJ

- MacLean, John. "Achievements." *JohnMacLean.com.au.* May 13, 2011. Accessed May 13, 2011. http://www.johnmaclean.com.au/ achievements.aspx#/site/DefaultSite/filesystem/images/galleria/ K4K_Bike_Ride_2002_2.jpg

- MacLean, John, with Paul Connelly. *Sucking the Marrow Out of Life.* Australia: Murdoch Books, 2005.

- Milgram, Stanley. "Behavioral study of obedience." *Journal of Abnormal and Social Psychology,* vol. 67 (1963): 371-378.

- Milgram, Stanley. *Obedience to Authority: An Experimental View.* New York: HarperCollins, 2004.

- "New Words." *Merriam-Webster.com.* Accessed March 20, 2011. http://www.merriam-webster.com/info/new_words.htm

- Peter, Laurence J. and Raymond Hull. *The Peter Principle: Why Things Always Go Wrong.* New York: Collins Business, 2009.

- "Population Below Poverty Line by Country." *NationMaster. com.* Access Date March 29, 2009. http://www.nationmaster. com/graph/eco_pop_bel_pov_lin-economy-population-below-poverty-line.

- Rath, Tom and Barry Conchie. *Strengths-Based Leadership: Great Leaders, Teams and Why People Follow."* New York: Gallup Press, 2008.

- Smith, Gordon H., sponsor. *A resolution expressing the sense of the Senate regarding the massacre at Srebrenica in July 1995.* Senate Resolution 134, 109th United States Congress. 2005.

- Stapert, Calvin. "To The Glory of God Alone." ChristianHistory. net. July 1, 2007. Accessed May 13, 2011. http://www.christiani-tytoday.com/ch/2007/issue95/1.8.html

- Tackett, Del. *Focus on the Family's The Truth Project.* Colorado Springs: Focus on the Family, 2004-2010.

- "The Holy Bible, New International Version." *Biblegateway.com.* Accessed April 2008-April 2011.

- "The Holy Bible, New International Version." *Biblegateway.com.* Accessed April 2008-December 2010.

- *The World Factbook 2009*. Washington, DC: Central Intelligence Agency, 2009. Access Date April 4, 2011. https://www.cia.gov/library/publications/the-world-factbook/index.html.

- Wallace, Lew. *Ben Hur: A Tale of The Christ*. New York: Harper & Brothers, 1901.

- Zimbardo, P. G (2007) "Understanding How Good People Turn Evil." *Democracy Now!* Interview Transcript: March 30, 2007. Access Date March 29, 2011. http://www.democracynow.org/2007/3/30/understanding_how_good_people_turn_evil.

- Zimbardo, P. G. *The Lucifer Effect: Understanding How Good People Turn Evil*. New York: Random House Trade Paperbacks, 2008.